Dedication

This book is dedicated to my lovely Mother, Ms. Larry. Mom, you are my role model, my rock, and my biggest cheerleader in life. Thank you for your support Mom. I love you.

Acknowledgements and Special Thanks

Special thanks to the following for their prayer, support, and encouragement for the success of this book:

Ms. Larry:
Thank you #1 Mom.

Dr. Jenice :
Thank you for being such a great mentor and for always leading by example.

Darlene Anderson-LeFlore:
Thank you for your outstanding editing of this book.

Sheery:
Thank you for being an awesome friend and spiritual advisor.

Charley:
Thank you for introducing me to this fabulous HR career and for being a great mentor!

Chad Barr:
Thank you for mentoring me this past year.

Veronica and Jessica:
Sister and niece, thank you for your support!

Marjorie and Lee:
Sister and nephew, thank you for your support!

Bennie, Bonnie, Bertha, and Lela:
My wonderful Aunts, thank you for your support!

Connie and Cynthia:
My wonderful cousins, thank you for your support!

Renee:
Thank you for being such a wonderful friend for 40-years!

Mr. Benning:
Thank you for your support!

In memory of:
Ms. Robin Dansby, Mr. Max Scott, and Mr. Andy Yuroff – I miss you.

Disclaimers

The contents and information contained in this book are meant as guidelines only. The characters are not representative of any particular real life person, place, or thing. Any similarities to real people, places, things, etc. are purely coincidental. The "fixes" are suggestions and recommendations. There are no guarantees or promises regarding the outcome of real life matters, situations, issues, cases, etc., related to and/or based on the contents contained in this book.

Additionally, the information contained in this book should not be construed as legal advice to be applied to any specific factual situation. If you are unsure whether your particular situation requires that a document, process, policy, procedure, etc., be changed, it is best to seek assistance from your HR Representative and/or consult your legal counsel.

Please note: If you have collective bargaining agreements, please consider your union contracts requirements when reading this book. Also, please remember to consider and abide by your local and state laws as you read and review this book.

Table of Contents

How to Use this Book

This book was written for your convenience. The mistakes are in no particular order. You are free to read the book from cover to cover, or, if you choose, you can thumb down the table of contents and read each mistake as needed. When reading this book, please always consider your union contracts, if applicable; as well as your local and state laws.

Forward
How God and Human Resources Saved My Life

After a long day, on the evening of September 22, 2016, I began working on a major project for a client. After completing the project around 12:30 a.m., I reclined in my favorite chair and began watching Investigative ID. I had planned to go to bed by 1:00 a.m.; but, I was so exhausted; I drifted off to sleep before 1:00 a.m.

At the time, I was the only person in the house; yet, I was awaken by two jabs to the back of my head. I quickly noticed that the object felt like hard steel, and I heard a man's stern voice say "Wake Up!" I suddenly realized that the "hard steel object" was a gun against my head! Even though I was jarred out of my sleep and a little confused, I knew to stay calm.

The man said "Don't look at me, don't turn around." I calmly replied, "Yes sir, what can I do for you sir?" His question, "How much money can you get out of the bank today?" I didn't know the answer to the question, but I knew not to stutter, so I said "$500." He said, "Good. Do you have anything on under there?" referring to the blanket I had covering me. He probably could sense that I was alarmed by his question and he quickly said "I don't want to have sex with you or anything." So to his question, I answered "No." (I did not have much on under the blanket). He said, "I want you to get dressed. We're going to the bank. I want your bank account. I want all the money!" I said, "Sir, I don't mind getting dressed and complying with your request, but I ask that you don't watch me get dressed." To my surprise, he said, "Ok, I will step back here and I won't watch you, but I will know what you are doing."

In preparation for the following day, I had laid my clothes out before I went to bed so they were easily accessible. I began to get dressed, all the while thinking and strategizing on how I would survive. It was dark in the room, but the TV gave off a little light. I could see my cell phone and was able to slip it in my pocket without him seeing me. After I got dressed, he said, "Okay, we are going out the back door." To this statement I replied, " Sir, I cannot go out of the back door, I have to go out of the front door." I made it sound as if I had a phobia about the back door. In actuality, I wanted to go out of the front door because it was much closer to where we were standing and there was a much longer way to the back door. He said, "Okay, we will go out the front door, and remember I am behind you! Oh yeah, I need your credit cards too."

As he followed closely behind me and we walked out the front door, I was constantly thinking about what I was going to do to survive this situation. Instantly I remembered watching a show on Investigative ID about a young woman who was kidnapped and was ordered to withdraw money from her bank ATM. After she withdrew the money, and gave it all to the thief, he killed her. I also remembered watching an episode of Oprah; the day she had a guest security expert on who said to never go to the second location with a criminal. These two things kept going through my mind, as well as the fear that my Mom, family, and friends would never know what happened to me.

When we got outside, and were close to my car, I began pushing the car's panic button and said, "Sir, you are going to have to kill me right here, because I am not going with you!" He started to tug on my blouse, and jerk on my arm. I started yelling as loud as I could "Helppppp Me!, Helpppppp! Somebody help me!!!" While I was yelling I began moving quickly toward the road (I lived on a busy road). My behavior of going from calm to crazy seemed to throw him off guard because the intruder seemed to panic and ran off. I was now safe. Ten days later the intruder was apprehended while robbing a nearby home.

I know that God and my human resources education, certification, experience, etc., allowed me to remain calm, think rationally, and strategize. Because, often times, when dealing with difficult HR issues, you have just one opportunity, to think and make the right decision.

Thank you God and HR.

Why I Wrote This Book

HI! My name is Vanessa G. Nelson. I am the founder, President and CEO of Expert Human Resources, founded in 2009 and located in Flint, Michigan. I have approximately 20 years of experience in human resources and started my company after realizing that most organizations were struggling with employment law compliance and HR regulations. Employers were being sued for obscene amounts of money, and /or were paying outrageous settlements as a result of litigation.

My mission and goal for this company has always been to protect organizations from lawsuit abuse and excessive compliance fees. I consider myself successful in my career and take pride in knowing that I have blocked many fees, lawsuits, settlements, etc. from taking form; by my estimation, $5 – 10 million dollars or more.

Human Resources is my passion and it's one of the reasons I get up each morning. I wish I could partner with every single organization in the United States to make sure they have the right policies, procedures, and processes in place. I yearn to tell employers about the importance of being compliant and consistent in applying policies and practices. **My desire is to show how it can hurt the organization when practices are not consistent with the law, as well as not aligned to company mission and goals. Unfortunately, I can't possibly work with every single organization; therefore, I decided to write this book.**

It is crucial that employers are familiar with the costly Human Resources mistakes that organizations make everyday, as well as the methods to fix them, BEFORE they become unmanageable. This book was written as a tool to help ensure organizations are as efficient as possible; because the real revenue often lies in efficiencies.

This book is filled with just a few of the experiences I've had over time throughout the United States. The names and locations have been changed, and situations scrambled to protect the innocent employers, employees, and businesses! I do hope that this book is helpful and will help you circumvent litigation and compliance headaches. If you find this book helpful, or not, I would love to hear about it. Please send me a message via my website, **http://www.experthumanresources.com.**

Thank you for your purchase. Happy reading to you!

Create Great Teams

When organizations fix the mistakes listed in this book, great teams can be created; which will be reflected in positive ways, including:

- *Improved morale*
- *Employee retention*
- *More funds available for staffing and employee programs*
- *Improved workflow*
- *Increased productivity*
- *Better communication and focus on organizational mission and goals*
- *Less stress*
- *Increased revenue!*

001 | UNDERESTIMATING HUMAN RESOURCES' **VALUE** TO THE ORGANIZATION

While consulting with employers, oftentimes comments are made that are dismissive to the value of Human Resources. Statements such as:

- "HR is not a revenue generating department, therefore it can be eliminated," or
- "We can put "Nancy" from Billing, or "Sally" the Receptionist, over HR," or
- "HR requires a low skill set, therefore, we can combine Tom's area with HR."

The comments go on and on. I can't stress enough how this way of thinking can negatively impact the success of your organization.

In the late 80's and early 90's, most human resources departments were known as "paper-pushing departments." A time where HR staff was responsible for the administrative duties, i.e., placing employment advertisements in the local papers, conducting employment testing, managing new hire paperwork, administering benefits, and so on; more of a reactive department. During the same timeframe, my employer's HR department was located in a trailer across the street from the company's headquarters. This is a prime example of the level of importance the company placed on their HR department.

The Mistake: The Human Resources department must be used as a vital strategic partner to the organization. Why? Because mistakes made in HR can be costly; compliance fees are expensive; and lawsuits, which are on the rise, can substantially negatively impact the organization's bottom line.

It is a huge mistake to not to realize that HR provides value via saving the company money in multiple ways, including:

- Avoiding litigation,
- Ensuring employment law compliance is maintained,
- Hiring the right people for the right jobs, and
- Working in synchronization with management regarding workplace issues.

The amount of money saved could be hundreds of thousands to millions of dollars in lawsuits, penalties, and fines!

Additionally, it is imperative that HR's value align with organizational goals, this can be accomplished by:

- **Creating great teams to promote competitiveness in an ever-changing global market.**
- Ensuring new hires can drive performance to impact the bottom line.
- Analyzing and offering benefits packages that attract high-quality workers.
- Training and developing managers and employees to ensure optimal operations and performance.
- Providing programs and systems to ensure employees are engaged and excited about their jobs.
- Developing retention programs to keep great people at the organization.

How to fix the mistake: HR should not be taken lightly. It should be utilized as a strategic partner to provide value. HR should be in close communication with management, as well as centrally located and convenient to management and employees. In other words, HR has earned a seat at the organizations' strategic planning table and is a vital part of the decision making process.

Still not convinced HR is valuable? Please know that it is crucial to change your prospective. Remember, without qualified HR staff and by not utilizing HR as a strategic partner; not only will operations suffer and competitiveness decrease; the organization could be heavily sued, fined, and/or penalized. Additionally, turnover could soar and morale could decline; eventually, the organization could go out of business; which would be an awful consequence to not recognizing HR's value.

Mistake

002 | NOT BUILDING A SOLID FOUNDATION

In my profession, I receive numerous calls from employers asking for help with problem employees. One conversation went something like this:

Employer - Chris is not performing well. Actually, she has never really performed well; she just does enough to get by. Lately her performance is so bad that I probably just need to fire her.

Me -
How long has Chris worked for your company?

Employer -
Oh, about 12 years.

Me -
Did Chris know what was expected of her?

And after many, many words and phrases from the employer, the answer is basically "No!"

The Mistake: The above scenario is definitely not good. It appears that the company knew, from the start, that this employee was a low performer. The mistake was prolonging dealing with the low performance issue. By allowing the problem to continue and fester, it most likely sent a message to the employee, and other employees, that this behavior was acceptable; and also depicted unacceptable behavior as a normal occurrence. Additionally, if the employer terminated the employee without prior warning, it could put the organization at risk of expensive litigation costs.

How to fix the mistake: Building a solid foundation could have eliminated this problem. Building a foundation is analogous to building a house. Okay, I have never built a house, but I know you have to put down concrete or some type of foundation, you have to build the walls, put in drywall, put on a roof, etc...All of these items are necessary before you start to paint, decorate, and move in; and Human Resources deserves just as much attention.

Before you require expectations from employees, you should build your foundation, which includes the following:

- Establishing policies, procedures, conduct rules, job descriptions, and processes that align with company mission, goals, and objectives.
- Ensuring employees are aware of the mission, policies, procedures, conduct rules, job descriptions, processes, etc.
- Orienting all new hires to this information.
- Reviewing policies and procedures with employees frequently.
- Providing feedback about employee performance early on; by discussing the problem and the expectations.
- Administering performance improvement plan processes accordingly.
- Following the policies and progressive disciplinary process consistently.

By building the HR foundation, low performance employees may not make it past the hiring process or at least past the first 90 days.

003 | **NOT** POSSESSING AN **EMPLOYEE HANDBOOK**
OR MAINTAINING POLICIES

t's surprising to me how many organizations don't possess employee handbooks. I once met with a client that had approximately 200 employees; yet they did not have an Employee Handbook. When asked why he didn't have an employee handbook, he stated that his lawyer told him that it was not necessary. He further stated that his lawyer said that if any issues arose, that he (the lawyer) would "get him out of it." Definitely Not! This statement makes my skin crawl still today.

The Mistake: Not having an employee handbook can be a costly decision for the employer, as the handbook is one of the most important communication tools at the organization. Not having one can cost the employer during litigation. Let me give an example: In 2011, the U.S. Equal Employment Opportunity Commission (EEOC) was victorious in a jury trial, in federal district court, returning a $1,260,080 verdict in a significant sexual harassment lawsuit brought by the EEOC. The verdict settled the EEOC's suit against a grocery store in Oswego, N.Y., and had charged that a class of female employees were subjected to a sexually hostile work environment by the store's general manager for more than 10 years.

The grocery store claimed, in its defense, that, while it didn't have an employee handbook, everyone knew how to use the owner's open-door policy to get help. However, that wasn't good enough for the court, which said the case should go to trial because the company failed to show it acted reasonably to prevent or stop the sexual harassment.

How to fix the mistake: Maintaining an employee handbook can help protect employers from litigation by showing that the employer had a clearly defined complaint procedure. The handbook should also detail how to issue/file a complaint, following the chain of commands. When I develop employee handbooks, I typically write an Anti-harassment Policy, Retaliation Policy, and include a complaint procedure; all located in the same area for ease of access.

Your handbook should also include:

- Disclaimers, i.e. not a contract, employment is not guaranteed, hours are not promised, etc.
- Company history/background
- Employment at-will (if applicable)
- Equal employment opportunity, harassment, non-discrimination policies
- Employee conduct, attendance policy, discipline process
- Pay day
- Benefits, vacation, sick, and/or Paid Time Off (PTO)
- Injury reporting, workers compensation
- Family and Medical Leave Act (FMLA)
- Work hours and meal breaks
- Social Media Policy
- Workplace violence and bullying
- Employee classifications
- Complaint process
- Accommodations
- Drug and alcohol free workplace
- Safety
- Emergency closings
- Dress code
- Computer and Internet usage

Employee handbooks should include clear language that is easy to read and understand. It is important to be careful with wording to ensure not to box in the employer. Handbooks should be written in different languages to meet the needs of employees.

What not to keep in the employee handbook: I highly recommend consulting with a human resources consultant or legal counsel to assist with the writing of the employee handbook. It is crucial not to include certain items in the handbook, because those items could cause employers problems. Some of the suggested topics not to include in the employee handbook are:

11

- Just cause. Unless you have a union contract requiring just cause or live in a state that requires it, please leave it out.
- Permanent position. Never, ever refer to "regular" employment positions as "permanent." It tends to create an expectation that employment is guaranteed; it may be "at-will."
- Due process. Never promise "due process" or anything similar for disciplinary actions or grievances (if applicable).
- Probationary period. Use the term "orientation," "introductory," or "trial" period instead. "Probationary" creates an expectation that the employee's status will change after he completes the period. It doesn't. The employee may still be employed "at will".

Important notes:

- Make sure that employees sign the "Acknowledgement of Employee Handbook." If they refuse to sign, have a witness verify and sign that they refused to sign the handbook.
- After creating the Employee Handbook, remember to distribute and review it with employees. By all means, don't leave the handbook on the shelf to collect dust (unfortunately, I've seen that before).

Mistake

LACK OF UNDERSTANDING

004 BASIC

EMPLOYMENT LAWS

Understanding basic employment laws is crucial to managing the organization. Ignoring employment laws can be detrimental to operations and costly in non-compliance fees and/or litigation.

The Mistake: Multiple and serious issues can occur simultaneously in the workplace. Many times, while conducting HR Audits for organizations, I uncover crucial issues that require I stop the audit to conduct a prompt investigation. During one such incident, an employee shared that he had been sexually harassed by a manager for almost a year. He told me that the manager constantly rubbed against him, and asked him out. The employee stated that although he told his manager he was married, she continued to harass him. He had complained to a few managers, but no one took him serious. The employee stated he was embarrassed because his guy friends told him to "suck it up" and that it was not a big deal. Well, the complaint was substantiated and I advised the client to take immediate disciplinary action.

Fortunately, the client dodged a bullet...(with my direction).

The incident could have been avoided if the managers had a basic understanding of employment laws. Issues such as this could have been addressed right away, and the employee may not have suffered harassment.

How to fix the mistake: Employers are inundated with legal compliance. Listed below are pertinent employment laws. **Please note: Employers are encouraged to become knowledgeable to local and state employment laws as well.**

Federal Employment Laws

The U.S. Department of Labor (DOL) is the authorized federal institution responsible for setting federal mandated employment laws. The Department of Labor (DOL) regulates more than 180 federal employment laws, which govern the occupational activities for employers and employees and implements and governs the workplace activities of approximately 10 million employers and 125 million employees. The laws also apply to job seekers, contractors, retirees, and grantees. The DOL enforces the laws to protect employment rights of job seekers and wage earners.

Fair Labor Standards Act (FLSA)
The Fair Labor Standards Act (FLSA) 29 U.S.C. 201 et. Seq., requires covered employers to pay the federal minimum wage and overtime, and sets child labor standards. FLSA also prohibits wage differences based on gender, requires employers to pay employees for time worked for the employer (that benefits

the employer) and sets the rules regarding workers younger than 18 years old.

Equal Pay Act
The Equal Pay Act, which is part of the Fair Labor Standards Act (FLSA), requires employers to provide equal pay and benefits to men and women who do the same or equivalent work, i.e. work that requires equal skill, effort, and responsibility. Job titles are not the deciding factor in whether two jobs are equal, that work duties and responsibilities are the determining factor.

Immigration Reform and Control Act (IRCA)
Immigration laws, enforced by the Bureau of US Citizenship and Immigration Services (USCIS), prohibit employers from hiring aliens who don't have government authorization to work in the United States.

Occupational Safety and Health Administration (OSHA)
The Occupational Safety and Health Act is a comprehensive law designed to reduce workplace hazards and improve health and safety programs for workers. It requires employers to provide a workplace free of physical dangers and to meet specific health and safety standards. Employers must also provide safety training to employees, inform them about hazardous chemicals, notify government administrators about serious workplace accidents, and keep detailed records.

Uniform Guidelines for Employee Selection Procedures
The Uniform Guidelines on Employee Selection Procedures are used by the EEOC, Department of Labor, Department of Justice, and Office of Personnel Management, to explain how an employer should deal with hiring, retention, promotion, transfer, demotion, dismissal, and referral. Under the uniform guidelines:

- Disparate impact occurs when protected-class members are substantially underrepresented in employment decision. It is determined by 4/5th's rule.
- Job-related validation means every factor used to make employment related decisions – recruiting, selection, promotion, termination, discipline, and performance appraisal – must be shown to be job related.

Uniformed Services and Re-Employment Rights Act (USERRA) of 1994

The Uniformed Services and Re-Employment Rights Act (USERRA) protects civilian job rights and benefits for veterans and members of the active and Reserve components of the U.S. armed forces. USERRA provides that returning service-members must be promptly reemployed in the same position that they would have attained had they not been absent for military service, with the same seniority, status and pay, as well as other rights and benefits determined by seniority.

Americans with Disabilities Act

The Americans with Disabilities Act (ADA) provides protection against discrimination of disabled individuals. Title I of the act prohibits discrimination in employment decisions against qualified individuals with a disability. A disabled person, to be qualified, must be able to perform the essential functions of the job with or without accommodation. The ADA covers individuals during the job application process, hiring, firing, promotion, compensation, selection for training, and any other terms, conditions, or privileges of employment. The act covers individuals who have a disability defined as:

- Having a physical or mental impairment that substantially limits one or more major life functions.
- Having a record of such impairment.
- Regarded or treated as having an impairment. (Phillips, 2006, 158)

On September 25, 2008, President Bush signed into law the American with Disabilities Amendment Act (ADAAA) of 2008, on January 1, 2009. This law is intended to clarify the ADA law and strengthen worker protections. The law will:

- Prohibit the consideration of measures that reduce or mitigate the impact of impairment – such as medication, prosthetics and assistive technology – in determining whether an individual has a disability.
- Include in the definition of a disability, those impairments that are episodic or in remission, if the medical condition would fall within the definition when active.
- Cover workers whose employers discriminate against them based on a perception that the worker is impaired, regardless of whether the worker has a disability.
- Clarify that the Americans with Disabilities Act provides broad coverage to protect anyone who faces discrimination on the basis of disability.

Title VII – Civil Right Act

Title VII of the Civil Rights Acts of 1964 prohibits discrimination in employment as follows:

It shall be unlawful employment practice for an employer –

- *To fail or refuse to hire or to discharge any individual or otherwise discriminate against any individual with respect to his compensation, terms, conditions, or privileges of employment, because of such individual's race, color, religion, sex, or national origin; or*
- *To limit, segregate, or classify his employees or applicants for employment in any way, which would deprive or tend to deprive any individual of employment opportunities or otherwise adversely affect his status as an employee, because of such individual's race, color, religion, sex, or national origin.*

The results of this act created protected classes, which are:

- Race
- Sex
- Religion
- National Origin
- Color
- Disabilities (Americans with Disabilities Act)
- Employees over 40 (Age Discrimination in Employment Act)
- Discrimination – EEOC also protects individuals from sexual harassment and retaliation

Pregnancy Discrimination Act (PDA)

The Pregnancy Discrimination Act makes it illegal to discriminate against a woman in any aspect of employment because of pregnancy, childbirth, or related medical conditions. Employers must treat pregnant women the same for all employment purposes, including fringe benefits, as other employees who are similar in their ability or inability to work.

Genetic Information Non-Discrimination Act (GINA)

Genetic Information Nondiscrimination Act (GINA) prohibits employers from discriminating on the basis of information derived from genetic tests.

Age Discrimination in Employment Act (ADEA)
The Age Discrimination in Employment Act (ADEA) prohibits discrimination against employees who are 40 years old or older. The act prohibits discrimination in hiring, promotion, compensation, retirement, layoff, discharge, and any other terms, conditions, or privileges of employment. Employers may not retaliate against employees for exercising their rights under the law.

COBRA – Consolidated Omnibus Budget Reconciliation Act (1985)
COBRA, Consolidated Omnibus Budget Reconciliation Act, requires employers to offer employees, former employees, or employee's family members the option of continuing health care coverage if their coverage is lost or reduced because: Their employment has been terminated for any reason, except gross misconduct; their hours have been reduced; or they have become eligible for Medicare.

Family and Medical Leave Act (FMLA)
The Family and Medical Leave Act (FMLA) became effective on August 5, 1993 for most employers and entitles eligible employees to take:

- Up to 12 weeks of unpaid, job-protected leave in a 12-month period for specified family and medical reasons;
- Up to 12 weeks of job-protected leave in the applicable 12-month period for any "qualifying exigency" arising out of the fact that a covered military member is on active duty, or has been notified of an impending call or order to active duty, in support of a contingency operation; or
- Up to take up to 26 weeks of job-protected leave in a "single 12-month period" to care for a covered service member with a serious injury or illness.

Worker Adjustment and Retraining Act (WARN)
The Worker Adjustment and Retraining Notification Act (WARN) protects workers, their families, and communities by requiring employers to provide notification 60 calendar days in advance of plant closings and mass layoffs. Employees entitled to notice under WARN include managers and supervisors, as well as hourly and salaried workers. Employers who violates the WARN provisions are liable to each employee for an amount equal to back pay and benefits for the period of the violation, up to 60 days.

005 | FAILURE TO TRAIN **MANAGERS PROPERLY**

About four years ago, while conducting an HR Audit for a large employer, I noted that many of the managers were performing their duties inconsistently and without direction. For example: Because the company had multiple sites, it was typical for a manager at one site to give a written warning or suspension to an employee for a rule violation; whereas a manager at a different site would overlook the issue. These inconsistencies could be seen as favoritism and/ or discrimination, which could be detrimental to the success of the organization.

The Mistake: When managers are not properly trained and prepared for workplace issues, companies could face discrimination suits, litigation, settlements, lawyer fees, unplanned expenses, employee turnover, morale issues, and a possible negative community image.

Additionally, the Equal Employment Opportunity Commission (EEOC) recommends training to confirm that companies are compliant with federal laws. The most recognized legal issue pertaining to the EEOC is sexual harassment in the workplace. The EEOC states: "Harassment violates federal law if it involves discriminatory treatment based on race, color, sex, religion, national origin, age, disability, genetic information, pregnancy, or any other protected characteristic." Under EEOC regulations, it is also a violation if harassment results from job discrimination opposition or participation in workplace investigations/complaint processes.

How to Fix the Mistake: Managers are the organization's first line of defense; they are on the front lines and interact with employees regularly. It is important to train managers to be on the lookout for inappropriate behavior, such as harassment, bullying, violent tendencies, etc

Managers should be trained regarding:

- Workplace policies and procedures.
- Basic employment laws.
- Anti-harassment and discrimination prevention.
- How to and when to conduct efficient workplace investigations.
- How to communicate with employees and have uncomfortable conversations with employees.
- Progressive discipline and documentation.
- The importance of utilizing HR for assistance with workplace issues.
- How to make decisions and when to move the problem to upper management.
- How to manage different generations.
- The difference between managing employees and bullying employees.

It is a good idea to use a third party to train managers; which can be a plus and viewed favorably if you are audited by a government agency or faced with litigation.

In the above example, training was provided for mangers who had not been involved in employment training sessions in over 10 years. The organization is now running well, like a "well-oiled machine".

006 NOT ANALYZING
JOB NEEDS
BEFORE HIRING

Last year, I ran into Joe at a networking event for one of the out-of-state chamber societies. Joe manages an organization with about 1,000 employees. He told me that he was having trouble with excessive new hire turnover. He shared that new hires "stayed about 2 months or 3 months and then left." I was surprised to hear this, as Joe's company appeared to be doing well. We talked for about an hour or so and our discussion led to my company performing an HR Audit to determine the root cause of the "new-hire turnover".

Well, it didn't take very long to reveal the issue...

The Mistake: Joe's HR Representative would receive a request to fill a position. For example, request to fill the Office Manager open position. The HR Representative would go to his computer; pull up the Office Manager job posting from the last Office Manger vacancy, post the position, interview, and hire the best candidate (per his opinion). You may be thinking, "what's wrong with that?" Well, the problem is the HR Representative did not communicate with the Director or Manager of the position to be filled. He just began working to fill the position, without really knowing exactly what the job entailed. It is also obvious that the HR Representative was not "at the table" for strategically planning the needs of the department. This mistake could easily cause the organization to make a "wrong" hire or bad hire, which could prove costly.

How to Fix the Mistake: The success of the organization is dependent upon employee performance. Not only should the HR

Representative be involved in strategic planning, the HR personnel should be in constant communication with managers and Directors regarding staffing requirements. Therefore, I highly recommend that employers conduct a job analysis for all jobs to be filled. Especially jobs that have not been filled within the past 2+ years, or where there has been high turnover.

According to Human Resources Management, a job analysis is the "systematic process of determining the skills, duties, and knowledge required for performing jobs in an organization." Conducting a job analysis helps to identify the tasks to be performed as part of the job duties. Traditionally, it is an essential and pervasive HR technique and starting point for other HR activities."

In today's rapidly changing work environment, the need for a sound job analysis system is critical. New jobs are being created, and old jobs are being redesigned or eliminated. A job analysis conducted only a few years ago may now be obsolete or restructured. A job analysis provides a summary of a job's duties and responsibilities, its relationship to other jobs, the knowledge and skills required, and working conditions under which its tasks are performed. (Mondy and Martocchio)

In summary, it is important to conduct a job analysis for open positions to:

• Review and evaluate the job tasks and responsibilities.
• Identify obsolete duties and add needed duties.
• Ensure the right people are recruited for the job and have the knowledge, skills, and ability to perform the job.
• Develop ADA (Americans With Disabilities Act) compliant job descriptions.

It is extremely important to have great knowledge of the job you are hiring for in order to avoid turnover.

Mistake

007

FAILURE TO CREATE A
JOB DESCRIPTION
FOR EACH JOB/POSITION
TO BE FILLED

I received an email from Pete, the former HR Director of a large corporation, requesting my assistance with establishing job descriptions. Pete shared that he was new in the role of Senior Vice-President for HR and realized that the job descriptions had not been updated for over 20 years. He stated the employees had basically recreated their jobs to their own likings over the 20 years and, at this point, he did not really know who was to be doing what. He was at his wits end because he was being challenged almost every time he delegated a task or project. I assured Pete that I could help him. Driving over 3 hours to meet with Pete, it was important to not only calm his nerves, but also to explain to him how I could help make his organization become more efficient.

The Mistake: *Having an outdated or insufficient job description is as bad as not having a job description at all.*

Risks of not having up-to-date ADA compliant job descriptions
If job descriptions are not updated or worse, don't exist; it could cost you massive fines when dealing with litigation. However, if your job descriptions are ADA Compliant and up-to-date, both are beneficial in court.

Job descriptions are one of the most important communication tools possessed by employers. Job descriptions inform employees of their job tasks, duties, and responsibilities. If job descriptions don't exist, employees rely on their own understandings of the job and oftentimes create their own duties and remove duties that may be crucial to the job. Pretty soon, it could have the same effect that "Pete" had.

Another mistake that I see is not having job descriptions for every job or not creating job descriptions for newly created jobs. It does not matter how simple or how advanced the job is; you need a job description. Possessing insufficient or outdated job descriptions, or no job descriptions at all, is likened to giving an employee an address 4 hours away (without a map or GPS) and telling them to find the address on their own. They will probably get lost, go in the wrong direction, and unfortunately, they may never find their way.

How to Fix the Mistake: It's pretty easy to determine how to fix
the mistake. You could start today by composing job descriptions or call an HR consultant (such as Expert Human Resources) for assistance and save time.

Benefits Of Possessing Up-To-Date Job Descriptions
An up-to-date, ADA compliant, job description is not only necessary to attract and recruit the best-qualified candidates for jobs; it is the foundation for most Human Resources functions. It is crucial that employees understand their job responsibilities and tasks; therefore, job descriptions are essential for:

- Highlighting the essential job functions of the job (ADA compliant)
- Training
- Performance evaluations and goals
- Compensation
- Benefits
- Performance management
- Workforce planning
- FMLA
- Workers' Compensation claims
- Litigation and Compliance Maintenance

Job Descriptions serve as a standard for other jobs. They can show how jobs interrelate. Therefore, it is extremely important to ensure your job descriptions are up-to-date.   It is recommended that job descriptions be reviewed and updated annually (at a minimum), or more frequently when situations arise.

A well-drafted job description includes:

- Position Title
- Who the Job Reports To

- Supervisory Responsibilities
- Department
- Fair Labor Standards Act (FLSA) Status
- Pay Grade
- Union (if applicable)
- Position Summary
- Essential Job Functions (core tasks)
- Non-Essential Job Functions
- Experience
- Education
- Knowledge, Skills and Abilities
- Physical Requirements
- Working Conditions
- Disclaimers

Mistake

008 | USING SOCIAL SECURITY **NUMBERS** ON PAPER JOB APPLICATION FORMS

It is surprising how many companies' still use paper applications and even more shocking how many of them ask for social security numbers, dates of birth, year of graduation, number of children, etc. As I think about it, in my experience, about 90% of paper applications have problematic questions or comments. While state laws vary on what information can be collected from applicants, and most states don't prohibit organizations from asking for social security numbers; I would advise to tread lightly with this issue.

The Mistake: Let me offer an example of one of the problems you could encounter by using the social security number on your paper job applications.

The scenario could be:

> John completes the job application for XYZ Company. John decides to hand deliver the job application. When John arrives to XYZ Company, he encounters Sally, Receptionist of XYZ Company. John asks Sally to please turn in his application to HR for him. Sally, the Receptionist, agrees and she takes the application inside with her. Sally almost forgets; however, she sees Bob, Janitor of XYZ Company, walking down the hall. Bob tells Sally that he's on his way to HR. Sally asks Bob if he would deliver the job application to HR since he's going there himself.

What's wrong with that scenario? Well, first of all Sally and Bob have access to John's social security number. And, at the time Sally takes possession of the application, XYZ Company is responsible for the social security number. If there was a case of identify theft, the employer could be responsible.

How to Fix the Mistake: It is a good idea to offer online applications that only reach HR Representatives and staff with a 'need to know' reason. However, if you are not able to offer an online solution, you could remove the social security number from the application and then only appropriate HR Representatives or staff should ask for the social security number when making an offer, conducting a background check, completing I-9 Forms, etc. I typically recommend that clients use a separate form to request this information, which is separate from the job application.

Additionally, organizations should have a process to destroy social security number information appropriately for applicants after making hiring decisions.

Mistake

009 | ASKING ILLEGAL INTERVIEW QUESTIONS

It's not uncommon for employers to utilize an interview team for hiring. What's surprising is how often the interview team has not been trained regarding illegal interview questions and how to interview candidates. I have conducted training on how to interview applicants and almost every time, someone in the class says, "Wow, I have been doing it wrong," or "I didn't know that was illegal."

The Mistake: Employers assign managers or other employees to interview potential employment candidates without considering the consequences of them asking illegal interview questions. An illegal interview question is one that seeks information the employer is not entitled to request and/or not entitled to use as a basis for job decisions. Most illegal questions cross the line by inquiring about protected characteristics, such as age, disability, race, or religion, which could be used to discriminate against the applicant.

How to Fix the Mistake: Interviewers should be trained to ask only job-related questions because it is unlawful under federal law not to hire candidates because of their race, color, sex (including certain protections for lesbian, gay, bisexual, and transgender (LGBT) individuals), religion, national origin, age, disability, genetic information, or military service. Some states also prohibit discrimination based upon marital status and other factors. Employers should avoid questions and conversation that could lead to discussion of these prohibited areas.

Sample Interview Questions to Avoid:

- Have you ever been arrested?
- Where were you born?
- I went to high school in Michigan, too—what year did you graduate?
- What is your religious affiliation?
- Have you made child care arrangements if you get this job?
- Have you ever been turned down for a job because of physical reasons?
- Do you have AIDS or any other infectious disease?
- Are you gay?
- What is your race?
- Are you pregnant?
- Have you ever brought a lawsuit against an employer?
- Have you ever filed for Workers' Compensation?
- Have you ever been sexually harassed?

Even if the interviewers' intentions are good, the consequences of asking inappropriate interview questions can lead to costly litigation. Employers should not assume that all interviewers know which questions are inappropriate. It could be as simple as a candidate stating they went to Disney Land and the interviewer asking "how many children do you have." This small comment could end up costly to the organization.

010 | MISREPRESENTING THE DETAILS OF JOB OPENINGS

One of my good friends, Jake, and I were talking one day. Jake mentioned to me that 5 years ago he was working for a great company where he was happy, and life was good. He said one day, out of the blue, an old acquaintance, Tom, called him and said he had a better opportunity for Jake. Even though Jake was happy, he was always open for better opportunities. Tom told Jake that the job was a higher-level position and it paid 60% more than Jake was currently making. Jake was very interested in the position and started getting really excited about this potential opportunity. Jake interviewed for the position and was hired. When Jake received his first paycheck, he noticed his pay was the same as his old job. He immediately went to Tom and said, "Hey, my check is short." Tom said, "No, your check is fine. I only told you that because you are a great employee and I wanted you to work here with us."

I don't have to tell you how Jake felt.

Also, I've sat in on interviews, where the interviewer tells the candidate inappropriate details about the job. For example, they may say "you will have a nice office," or "the staff gets along great together," or "we will give you an assistant," and on and on. All of which were not true.

The Mistake: Misrepresenting jobs you want to fill is bad business ethics. It can quickly damage organizations' reputations. I know you have heard the adage; bad customer service spreads 10 times as fast as good customer service. Well it's the same way with misrepresenting jobs. Quality candidates may not even apply to your job openings after hearing about your unethical practices.

How to Fix the Mistake: Be as honest as you can about the job responsibilities and expectations. If the office is small and cold, let the candidate know, but you can also tell them you will supply a heater and work on getting better space for them in the future. It is always best to be truthful. The candidate may not take the job if conditions are bad, however if they do accept the job offer, you know you have a dedicated employee; which is a lot better than dealing with bad reviews and/or expensive turnover.

011 | HASTILY HIRING **CANDIDATES** OR **MISTAKENLY** HIRING THE WRONG PERSON

While working closely with an organization, the CEO, Barbara, shared that it was extremely difficult to find and hire quality Certified Nurse Assistants (CNAs). She stated the company had begun the practice of hiring anyone who applied for the jobs, that met the requirements; and further stated that, in most cases the staff was ordered to hire them right on the spot. Well guess what, Barbara's organization was suffering with excessive turnover, caused mostly by terminations. Many of the CNAs did not last through the trial period of three (3) months. Even worse, due to high turnover, the organization would sometimes retain the "bad employees" simply to ensure staff availability and coverage. Big Problem!

Can you imagine a bad employee taking care of your ailing parent? How long would it be before you initiate a lawsuit for negligent hiring and/or negligent retention? I explained to Barbara this practice was definitely not a good idea.

The Mistake: The mistake is most likely obvious to you. Not doing your due diligence to ensure your new hire is a quality-hire, one who can hit the ground running; versus retaining bad hires, is not a smart way to manage staffing. Imagine the costs associated with this practice if continued over time.

Cost Of Turnover and/or a Wrong Hire

Wrong hires, i.e., employees who voluntarily quit, as well as terminated employees, must be replaced; this causes turnover. The costs associated with turnover can be twice the annual salary, depending upon the position. Because human capital plays a key role in the outcome of an organizations' financial performance, it can cause a negative impact to the bottom line.

The table below represents the approximate costs to hire an employee. The costs are estimated (calculated at a minimal amount) and based on the position of Certified Nurse Assistant.

CALCULATING WRONG HIRE REPLACEMENT AND TURNOVER COSTS

Cost of Attracting Applicants (advertisements, online posting, etc.)	$3,000
Pre-employment Administrative Expenses (paperwork, scheduling interviews, phone calls, background checks, etc.)	$200
Cost of interviews (cost of time involved for staff to interview)	$500
Cost of testing	$100
Cost of hiring decision meetings	$200
Cost associated with job orientation	$500
Cost of overtime to cover vacancy	$4,000
Cost of new employee training	$300
Cost of lost customers, sales, profits, etc.	$3,000
Cost of Unemployment Claims ($200/week for 6 months or 24 weeks)	$4,800
COSTS COULD BE	$16,600

In the above example, the costs could be in excess of $16,600 by hiring the wrong person and/or associated with employee turnover. Therefore, it is imperative to hire and retain the right people for the right jobs the first time. Special note: It costs even more to retain bad hires.

How to Fix the Mistake: It is not that difficult to fix this issue. I will give you 10 suggestions to decrease turnover:

- Audit your hiring process to make sure it is efficient and effective.
- Conduct a job analysis of the open position to ensure the job description provides an accurate depiction of the job responsibilities.
- Restructure the job, if possible to make it more attractive to new hires.

- Conduct background checks and reference checks.
- Revise the orientation and onboarding process.
- Offer perks, such as flexibility, 10-hour shifts, shared shifts, etc. (where possible).
- Encourage regular feedback, provide constructive criticism, and praise when appropriate.
- Incorporate an "open door" policy of management; especially for new hires.
- Ensure new hires have the tools they need to do their jobs; offer job shadowing or training.
- Only hire quality employees.

It takes time to fix the problem, but it will be well worth it in the long run.

Mistake

MAKING HIRING
012 | DECISIONS
BASED ON IMPROPER CRITERIA

I remember when Sally stated that she had a sensitive situation regarding a candidate that she and her team wanted to hire. Sally explained that everyone truly liked the candidate but the candidate had a slight accent. She further indicated that the customers might find the candidate's accent to be problematic or even offensive.

Over the years, I've heard all types of excuses to not hire certain applicants. Excuses such as:

- "I only hire tall, skinny, brunettes."

- " I have never had any luck hiring minorities so I don't consider them (for hire) anymore." Yes, someone actually said that to ME.
- "I don't consider candidates with any tattoos or piercings.
- "We have enough old people around here and we need to hire younger folk with energy."

Unbelievable right? You would be surprised how often this happens.

The Mistake: Title VII of the Civil Rights Act protects individuals against employment discrimination because of race, color, origin, gender, or religion. State laws typically cover even more protected classes. For example, the Michigan Elliott-Larsen Civil Rights Act also covers age, sex, height, weight, familial status, and marital status. Some states cover sexual orientation and transgender. This protection is intended to ensure that all employees and potential employees are presented with the same opportunities.

It's acceptable for employers/interviewers to follow their gut instincts regarding hiring decisions; but only to a certain point. Making decisions based on inappropriate criteria can be considered discriminatory, and simply put, illegal. Employers could be walking into dangerous territory if they look for reasons not to hire a candidate, when it is not job related, or based on a business necessity. These decisions can easily lead to expensive litigation.

How to Fix the Mistake: I don't want to sound like a broken record, however, training is essential to ensure that interviewers know not only how to interview and ask the right questions, but also the appropriate criteria to determine who to hire. Below are steps to help ensure that the interview and selection processes are appropriate:

- Interviewer(s) should review and gain a clear understanding of the organization's mission, goals, visions, and values.
- Employers should make certain that a job analysis is conducted for each position and that the essential job functions are clearly defined in the job description. This step should be completed prior to posting the position.
- Interviewer(s) should review the job description and ensure that he or she has a clear understanding of the job requirements.
- If a certain type of individual has to be hired due to a business necessity, make sure the business necessity is explained, well-defined, and documented prior to the interviews. Please note: There can be a thin line

between business necessity and discrimination.

- Interviewer(s) should use separate forms, such as an evaluation form, to ensure that the information gathered from candidates does not affect the decision-making process. I recommend that the interviewer(s) complete the evaluation form immediately after each interview; in order to evaluate each candidate on his or her own merit.
- Employer/interviewer(s) must be consistent with the application of hiring practices.

The goal is to be consistent and base hiring decisions on non-biased, job-related, appropriate criteria.

Mistake

013 | NOT CONSIDERING CANDIDATES WITH DISABILITIES
W H E N   H I R I N G

John, the HR Director of a transportation company, told me a great story about a man who applied for a big rig driver position at his company. John said, not only was the man only 4'8" tall, he had one leg. John said when the man walked into his office for an interview, he was very surprised at the man's appearance. John thought there was no way this man would be considered for the job.

As John went through the motions of conducting an interview, he found himself becoming very impressed by the candidate. At the end of the interview, John asked the candidate those famous words, "How would you perform the essential functions of this job?" The man explained to John his view of the process and then went so far as to tell John that he could show him. John took him out to a big rig and was amazed at how this man could get into the vehicle and drive it! Needless to say the man was hired.

This is an awesome story with a great ending. Unfortunately, employers do not always give disabled candidates a chance, especially when the disability is visible.

The Mistake: Oftentimes, employers want to avoid hiring the disabled with the thought it could raise healthcare benefits costs and create headaches in making accommodations. Unless there is a business necessity, this may be illegal, because the Americans with Disabilities Act (ADA) provides protection against discrimination of disabled individuals. Title I of the act prohibits discrimination in employment decisions against qualified individuals with a disability. A disabled person, to be qualified, must be able to perform the essential functions of the job, with or without an accommodation. The ADA covers individuals during the job application process, hiring, firing, promotion, compensation, selection for training, and any other terms, conditions, or privileges of employment.

The mistake is when employers don't take the time to do their due diligence in determining if the person with the disability is able to perform the essential functions of the job. Therefore, when employers/interviewers are not clear regarding the essential functions of the jobs, the hiring process oftentimes fails.

How to Fix the Mistake: Employers should conduct job analysis for positions they plan to fill. Job descriptions should be reviewed and updated to include clearly defined essential functions. When interviewing applicants with disabilities, be sure not to ask illegal interview questions. Treat each applicant the same and with consistency. If you become concerned about an applicant being able to complete the work tasks, you may ask, "How would you perform the essential tasks of the job for which you applied?"

Also, employers should provide reasonable accommodations, as appropriate, if the applicant is qualified, able to perform the essential tasks of the job (with or without accommodations), and is chosen for the job.

Mistake

014 | P O S S E S S I N G
INVALID
EMPLOYMENT TESTS

I was in the process of conducting an HR Audit for Brenda's company. While reviewing the hiring process, I noticed the tests appeared to be unrelated to the jobs. I also noticed that 95% of the employees that worked for the company looked the same, i.e. same race, around the same age, etc. I contacted Brenda and asked her where she obtained the employment tests. She told me the HR Generalist wrote the tests.

Continuing the HR Audit, I noticed that the company was located in an area with 47% Hispanic residents, yet there were no Hispanics working at her company. When I asked why, I was told that that Hispanics could not pass the test.

Is this a problem? Yes it most definitely is...

The Mistake: The mistake is not ensuring the employment tests are valid. The Civil Rights Act of 1964 established that employment decisions based on race, color, religion, sex, or national origin are discriminatory and illegal. In 1978, the Civil Service Commission, the Department of Labor, the Department of Justice, and the Equal Opportunity Commission jointly adopted the **Uniform Guidelines on Employee Selection Procedures (UGESP)** to establish uniform standards for employers for the use of selection procedures and to address adverse impact, validation, and record-keeping requirements.

Adverse Impact
Under the UGESP, adverse impact is a substantially different rate of selection in hiring, promotion or other employment decision; which

works to the disadvantage of members of a race, sex or ethnic group. A rule of thumb has been adopted under which it will generally consider a selection rate for any race, sex, or ethnic group which is less than four-fifths (4/5ths) or eighty percent (80%) of the selection rate for the group with the highest selection rate as a substantially different rate of selection.

Further, the UGESP defines selection procedures to include the following: any measure, combination of measures, or procedure used as a basis for any employment decision. Selection procedures as defined by the UGESP include the full range of assessment techniques, including written exams, performance tests, training programs, probationary periods, interviews, reviews of experience or education, work samples, and physical requirements. For more information: http://uniformguidelines.com/questionandanswers.html.

How to Fix the Mistake: Employers can fix this mistake by applying best practices for testing and selection, including:

- Administering tests and other selection procedures without regard to race, color, national origin, sex, religion, age (40 or older), or disability.
- Ensuring the test is valid and actually job-related or needed for a business necessity. Please note, while a test vendor's documentation supporting the validity of a test may be helpful, the employer is still responsible for ensuring that its tests are valid under UGESP.
- If a selection procedure screens out a protected group, the employer should determine whether there is an equally effective alternative selection procedure that has less adverse impact and, if so, adopt the alternative procedure.
- Ensure that tests and selection procedures are not adopted casually by managers who know little about these processes.
- Employer should be aware that not following the UGESP could prove to be a costly mistake.

Mistake

015 | MISCLASSIFYING
WORKERS
AS INDEPENDENT
CONTRACTORS

Don, the Dentist wanted to fire his dental hygienist, but he wanted to make sure he was processing the termination correctly. I asked Don why he was firing the employee and he replied, "Because she is rude to patients, is having absenteeism problems, and has a chip on her shoulder." He further commented that, "The rumor is, she's mad at me because I purchased a new Mercedes and she feels like she is not being paid enough." So starts the review of Don's dental practice.

I quickly realized that Don was violating the Fair Labor Standards Act (FLSA) by paying employees as independent contractors. Upon further inquiry, Don was wrongfully paying ALL of the workers as independent contractors, including the Receptionist. Because this was a crucial issue, I immediately stopped the review and asked Don his explanation for categorizing each employee as an independent contractor. Don's reply, "I don't like to deal with payroll and taxes or any of that stuff, so I pay them all as contractors and just pay them for their hours."

BIG Problem...

The Mistake: Employers usually classify workers as independent contractors to avoid:

• Paying expensive taxes, including social security and Medicare taxes.
• Paying overtime.
• Providing benefits.
• Dealing with unemployment and paying unemployment claims.
• Dealing with and paying for workers compensation insurance.

According to statistics, misclassifying workers costs the government $2.72 billion each year. It is predicted that 30% of employers using independent contractors misclassify them. The IRS has partnered with the DOL, hired additional investigators, and increased the budget, to "crackdown" on employers who misclassify workers.

Is it worth the risk? The consequences of misclassifying workers as independent contractors are:

- Since the employer failed to withhold income taxes, the employer faces penalties of 1.5% of the wages, plus 40% of the FICA taxes (social security and Medicare) that were not withheld from the employee and 100% of the matching FICA taxes the employer should have paid. Interest is also accrued on those penalties daily, from the date they should have been deposited.
- A Failure to Pay Taxes Penalty equal to 0.5% of the unpaid tax liability for each month up to 25% of the total tax liability.
- If the IRS suspects fraud or intentional misconduct, it can impose additional fines and penalties. For instance, the employer could be subjected to penalties that include 20% of all of the wages paid, plus 100% of the FICA taxes, both the employee's and employer's share **Criminal penalties of up to $1,000 per misclassified worker and 1 year in prison can be imposed as well.**
- $50 for each Form W-2 that the employer failed to file because of classifying workers as an independent contractor.
- In addition, the person responsible for withholding taxes could also be held personally liable for any uncollected tax.

Per the U.S. Department of Labor (DOL), Wage and Hour Division's (WHD), website: **https://www.dol.gov/whd/media/press/whdpressVB3. asp?pressdoc=national/20141002.xml,** in Fiscal Year 2013, WHD investigations resulted in more than $83,051,159 in back wages for more than 108,050 workers in industries, such as janitorial, food, construction, day care, hospitality, healthcare, and garment. WHD regularly finds large concentrations of misclassified workers in low-wage industries.

How to Fix the Mistake: Employers should have knowledge and
understanding of the FLSA law in order to classify independent contractors correctly. Independent contractors are self-employed individuals who offer their services to the general public, i.e. Plumbers, Accountants, Consultants, etc. Independent contractors receive a Form 1099-MISC at the end of each year that they are paid $600 or more that year.

One method to determine if a worker is an employee or an independent contractor, is a 3-point category test, which is based on:

1. **Behavioral Control –** Does the payer have the right to direct or control how the worker performs specific tasks?
2. **Financial Control –** Is the worker too dependent on the payer's

business to make a living?

3. **Type of Relationship** – How does the payer and the worker perceive the relationship?

There is also the IRS 20-Point Factor test that employers can access in the IRS Worker Classification Pamphlet at the IRS website: **https://www.irs.gov/pub/irs-utl/x-26-07.pdf.**

If, after reviewing the three categories of evidence, it is still unclear whether a worker is an employee or an independent contractor, employers can complete and file **Form SS-8**, Determination of Worker Status for Purposes of Federal Employment Taxes and Income Tax Withholding (PDF) with the IRS. The IRS will review the facts and circumstances and officially determine the worker's status. You can find the form at the website, **https://www.irs.gov/pub/irs-pdf/fss8.pdf.**

Typically the IRS finds out about violations in this area via:

- Disgruntled employees who may be angry that an independent contractor who may work next to them makes more money or has more freedoms.
- Independent contractors who are audited may cause inquiries involving your organization.
- Surprise audits from the DOL, IRS or other government agency.

Misclassifying workers as independent contractors is serious business and can be extremely costly. Therefore, I recommend that you review all of your independent contractors' contracts and job duties to make sure classifications are correct; before its too late.

Mistake

016 | MISCLASSIFYING WORKERS
A S   E X E M P T

I had just finished parking when Greg, CEO of a mid-sized company, summoned me over for a quick conversation. He said, "The Feds called and I am going to be audited. They told me they would be here next Wednesday and that they wanted to see my payroll sheets and pay practice information." I could hear the worry and anxiety in his voice. Because he was so upset, I decided to give him my immediate attention.

Greg liked to hire his "friends" for positions. I cautioned him against this practice earlier, but he told me that he trusted his friends and many of them had been with him for over10 years or from the inception of the company. It had been a while since I talked to Greg; therefore, I asked him if he had any idea why he was being audited. He listed several possibilities, however, one particular thing stood out; he had hired his friend 6 months ago. This was a serious red flag.

I asked Greg to tell me about his friend's position. He indicated that his friend was hired to supervise a process and was classified as an exempt employee. I asked Greg did the friend supervise anyone. Greg answered, "No".

Of course, the audit revealed that an employee on the payroll was misclassified as exempt. The Auditors ordered Greg to pay back wages, fines, and penalties for the error. Guess who was awarded payment of back wages? If you guessed Greg's friend, then you are correct. Coincidence? Maybe, maybe not.

The Mistake: This mistake is a common one. Misclassifying an employee as exempt is something I regularly encounter while performing an HR Audit. Oftentimes the error is caused by the employer simply not taking the time to review the position and exempt criteria before making classification decisions.

Recently, FLSA cases hit a record high. There were 8,954 cases filed between January 1, 2015 and December 31, 2015. The chart below shows the succession of increases in claims each year, i.e. 888 claims filed in 1990 to a record 8,954 claims filed in 2015.

FLSA Cases Filed by Calendar Year

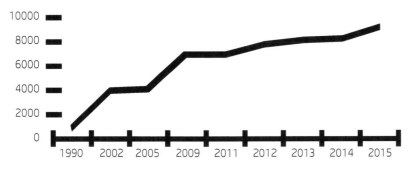

41

The Department of Labor estimates that 70% of employers are violating the FLSA in some way and have increased their budget to "crack down" on violators.

Consequences of Classifying Employees as Exempt

The consequences of classifying employees as exempt are:

- Payment of back wages.
- Fines of up to $1,100 per violation in the case of willful or repeated violations of minimum wage and overtime provisions.
- Injunctions preventing the sale, delivery, transportation, or shipment of goods produced by employees in violation of the law.
- **Criminal convictions: Employers may be fined up to $11,000 for a first conviction and up to $11,000 and/or imprisoned up to six (6) months for a second conviction.**
- Loss of exemptions for all employees in the classification or employees under the manager who misclassified the employees.

How to Fix the Problem: Management in charge of assigning classifications, i.e., HR Director, COO, Owner, Manager, etc., should be trained regarding the Categories of Exemption and Criteria as well as the definitions of exempt versus non-exempt, i.e. Examples include, Exempt Employees – Employees who meet one of the FLSA exemption tests and who are paid on a fixed salary basis, not entitled to overtime. Non-Exempt Employees – Employees who do not meet any one of the FLSA exemption tests and are not paid on an hourly basis and covered by wage and hour laws regarding minimum wage, overtime pay, and hours worked.

Categories of Exemption Criteria (the information below is sourced from the U.S. Department of Labor Fact Sheet#17A)

1. **Executive Exemption**
   - Employee must be compensated on a salary basis.
   - Employee's primary duty must be managing the enterprise, or managing a customarily recognized department or subdivision of the enterprise.
   - Employee must customarily and regularly direct the work of at least 2 or more other full-time employees or the equivalent; and
   - Employee must have authority to hire or fire other employees; or the employee's suggestions and recommendations as to the hiring, firing, advancement, promotion or any other change in status of other employees must be given particular weight.

2. **Administrative Exemption**
   - Employee must be compensated on a salary or fee basis.
   - Employee's primary duty must be the performance of office or non-manual work directly related to the management or general business operations of the employer or the employer's customers; and
   - Employee's primary duty includes the exercise of discretion and independent judgment with respect to matters of significant.

3. **Professional Exemption**
   - To qualify for the learned professional employee exemption, the following tests must be met:
     a. Employee must be compensated on a salary or fee basis.
     b. Employee's primary duty must be the performance of work requiring advanced knowledge, defined as work which is predominantly intellectual in character and which includes work requiring the consistent exercise of discretion and judgment;
     c. The advanced knowledge must be in a field of science or learning; and
     d. The advanced knowledge must be customarily acquired by a prolonged course of specialized intellectual instruction.
   - To qualify for the creative professional employee exemption, all of the following tests must be met:
     a. Employee must be compensated on a salary or fee basis.
     b. Employee's primary duty must be the performance of work requiring invention, imagination, originality or talent in a recognized field of artistic or creative endeavor.

4. **Computer Employee Exemption**
   - Employee must be compensated either on a salary or fee basis,
   - Employee must be employed as a computer systems analyst, computer programmer, software engineer, or other similarly skilled worker in the computer field performing the duties described below;
   - Employee's primary duty must consist of:
     a. The application of systems analysis techniques and procedures, including consulting with users, to determine hardware, software or system functional specifications;
     b. The design, development, documentation, analysis, creation, testing or modification of computer systems or programs, including prototypes, based on and related to user or system design specifications;
     c. The design, documentation, testing, creation or modification of computer programs related to machine operating systems; or
     d. A combination of the aforementioned duties, the performance of which requires the same level of skills.

5. **Outside Sales Exemption**
   - Employee's primary duty must be making sales (as defined in

the FLSA), or obtaining orders or contracts for services or for the use of facilities for which a consideration will be paid by the client or customer; and

- Employee must be customarily and regularly engaged away from the employer's place or places of business.

6. **Highly Compensated Employee Exemption**
   - Highly compensated employees performing office or non-manual work and paid total annual compensation are exempt from the FLSA if they customarily and regularly perform at least one of the duties of an exempt executive, administrative or professional employee identified in the standard tests for exemption.

I did not list the amount of compensation required above because at the time of writing this book the amounts were due to change. Please check the DOL website for the current compensation amounts.

Employers who misclassify employees as exempt can suffer costly fines, penalties, and litigation. Therefore, it is recommended that you review your exempt classifications to ensure they meet the standards of exemption criteria.

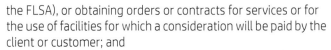

Mistake

017 | FAILURE TO CONDUCT **APPROPRIATE** REFERENCE CHECKS

I worked with a mid-size company that never conducted reference checks. The HR team checked criminal backgrounds, sex offender status, etc. but not references. I asked why and was told the organization believed in second changes and did not conduct reference checks. They wanted to give new hires a fresh start.

Well, while still consulting there, one day Jill got very angry with her coworker. She grabbed her co-worker and physically beat her. It took several people to pull Jill off of her coworker. The coworker was injured, which required immediate medical attention.

After conducting a little research about the employee, it was discovered that Jill had a history and a pattern of serious altercations with staff and management at previous companies. We uncovered Jill's past altercations in 10 minutes.

The Mistake: Jill could have seriously injured her co-worker or worse. Although it may be honorable for employers to offer second chances, it is best to check references. Reference checks can disclose embezzlement, bad attitudes, confirm workers' past work history listed in their resume/application, etc. Most of all, references can protect employers against the possibilities of incurring unnecessary expensive negligent hiring lawsuits.

How to Fix the Mistake: Negligent hiring typically occurs when an employer fails to check an employee's background (including references) and the employee injures someone. There is a potential negligent hiring practice when: 1) the employer hired an unfit employee who injures others, 2) the employer did an inadequate background check, or 3) the employer failed to find facts that would have led to rejection because of potential risk. Therefore if the employer knew or should have known, the employer could be liable. This is why it is important for employers to conduct reference checks. (Mathis)

Reference checks should include verification of employment with companies listed in the candidates' resume and/or application, as well as information about past performance. Reference checks should be conducted via former employers, i.e. managers, supervisors, senior leadership; not personal references, such as friends and family.

Employers should be meticulous in conducting reference checks on every employee to avoid negligent hiring litigation.

018 | COMPENSATION PLAN DOES NOT
EXIST OR IS NOT
ALIGNED
TO COMPANY GOALS

I was hired to recruit an Operations Coordinator for an organization with 10 offsite locations. The CEO placed certain salary restrictions on the position. After completing my portion of the recruitment, I forwarded five (5) recommendation candidates to the CEO and his team for their review. The team made the decision to make an offer to the candidate named Bob. The CEO requested to meet alone with Bob before making an official offer. This practice is not typical, however, the CEO told me he always liked to meet with the chosen candidate one more time, before finalizing things.

I later discovered that the CEO used that last meeting to negotiate a salary with the candidate. The conversation went something like this, the CEO would ask, "so how much money do you want?" In Bob's case, Bob threw a big number out there and the CEO agreed with Bob's salary request.

No problem right? Wrong.

The above situation was a huge problem because Bob's starting salary was higher than all of the Operations Coordinators at the other locations; some had been at the company for over 10 years. It appeared that Bob's compensation was higher simply because he was a better negotiator than the others.

The Mistake: Below are four mistakes employers make regarding compensation plans:

- **Not having a compensation plan:** Employers who want to succeed in the increasingly competitive environment must have a well-designed compensation plan that motivates employees; controls compensation costs, and ensures equity.
- **Not considering the organizations' mission and culture when developing the compensation plan:** The best compensation plans mirror the culture of the company. Employers should establish a compensation philosophy. Benefits programs should also be part of a company's compensation strategy.
- **Different gender pay for similar positions:** The Equal Pay Act requires that men and women in the same workplace be given equal pay for equal work. The jobs don't have to be identical, but they must be substantially equal. Job content (not job titles) determines whether jobs are substantially equal. If there is an inequality in wages between men and women, employers could suffer huge fines and penalties for non-compliance as well as potential litigation. Note: There may be exceptions for seniority, higher education, etc.
- **Unfair compensation plan:** Not conducting a comparable market study and research to ensure compensation plans are fair can not only cause compensation division, it can also result in wage disparities, disgruntled employees, low employee morale, and costly lawsuits.

How to Fix the Mistake: Maintaining an appropriate compensation plan can be one of the most important practices in attracting, hiring, and retaining great candidates and employees. Paying employees fairly is crucial to your organization. If you pay too little, your key employees may leave, and if you pay too much, you could drastically reduce profitability. Your compensation plan stands front and center. Compensation plans promote fairness and facilitates the ability to evaluate performance.

Employers should take the time to review position classifications and compensations, conduct a comparable market survey, and develop a compensation program. This process can be outsourced to professional HR firms that are well versed in all areas of developing and designing compensation programs. Compensation plans can help protect your company from expensive litigation as well as avoidance from fines and penalties for non-compliance of the law.

Mistake

019 | LACK OF ADMINISTERING
ADEQUATE JOB OFFER LETTERS
TO NEW HIRES

Over the years, I've reviewed a lot of Offer Letters of Employment and they come in all types and varieties. I clearly recall one offer letter because it was so poorly written. To my recollection, it read something like this:

"You are hired at XYZ Company. Your start date is January 1, 2010. Please report to Mr. Smith at 9:00 a.m. Welcome aboard!"

Seriously, that was it. That was the extent of the whole job offer letter! If it appears to be fine to you, then please call me...

The Mistake: New hires that do not receive adequate job offer letters could be confused about their jobs; and, if they are confused, it could lead to misunderstandings and miscommunications. New hires may think one thing and employers may mean another. The terms and intent of the job may be different. Confused new hires may seek clarification from their co-workers who, in many cases, can make matters worse. Co-workers often receive the wrong information and provide their own interpretations or, they may be disgruntled thinking that the new hire was offered more opportunities or pay than they received. What a mess this could become.

How to Fix the Mistake: Administering a well-written Offer Letter of Employment to new hires is important for many reasons:

- It is the organizations' opportunity to shine as it is a first impression of the organization;
- It allows the organization to outline the terms and conditions of the offer;

48

- Allows disclaimers and defines the at-will policy (if applicable);
- Describes compensation, benefits, and classification of the position;
- To ensure contingencies regarding background checks, reference checks, drug screen, physicals, etc. are detailed.

It is a good idea to require the new hire to sign the offer letter, typically within 5 – 10 days of the offer. The offer letter should also be witnessed by the HR Representative or other appropriate management staff of the organization.

Mistake

020 | LACK OF APPROPRIATE
ORIENTATION
AND ONBOARDING PROCESS

While auditing a human resources department in a non-profit organization, I discovered a turnover of staff. As part of the audit, I spent time with the HR Manager, Jack. Jack and I discussed the HR practices, processes, systems, policies, etc. One day Jack told me that he had orientation planned for that afternoon. I asked if I could sit in on the orientation and he said "of course!"

I planned on spending pretty much all afternoon in orientation with Jack; however, to my surprise, employee orientation took about 15 minutes. Jack gave the employees a few tax forms; the employee application, and a direct deposit slip to fill out. Lastly, he took a copy of their IDs. That was it...no offer letter, no job description, no handbook...nothing else. Afterwards, I asked Jack if a more formal orientation program was scheduled for a later date and he said, "No, that was it." Needless to say, I quickly realized one of the reasons for the turnover.

The Mistake: According to a 2012 survey conducted by Allied Workforce Mobility Survey, companies lose 25% of all new employees within the first year. The survey further indicated that the average cost to fill one position was about $11,000. If the position is a management, senior level, or hard-to-fill position, that cost could exceed one-year annual salary. The mistake of enduring this wasted expense, time and time again, due to turnover of staff, is excessive and so unnecessary.

Employee Orientation – Not appropriately orienting an employee to the organization is a lost opportunity to amplify on the excitement of the new hire. Its like missing a chance to showcase your great organization, and to introduce the new hire to the staff, as well as make new hires feel a part of the team.

Onboarding – Lack of providing a more socialized approach to acclimate the new hire to the culture of the organization is a missed opportunity. Not Ensuring that the new hire has the tools he or she needs to succeed; making sure they know their way around the organization; and ensuring that he or she knows where to go for questions, is a mistake because the new hire may feel like they don't "fit in," and most likely won't feel comfortable with the company or in the position.

How to Fix the Mistake: An effective orientation and onboarding

process is crucial to new hire success. Orientation allows the new hire to gain an understanding and excitement about the position. An effective employee orientation program has an agenda, which may include:

- The history/background of the organization.
- Introductions to Senior Leaders, Managers, and staff as appropriate.
- Assigning a "buddy."
- Benefits explanations.
- Safety presentation.
- Confidentiality program.
- Review of the employee handbook.
- Etc....

It is very important to take the time to develop an effective orientation and onboarding program, because it can be expensive to the organization without them.

Mistake

021 | NOT ENSURING NEW HIRES HAVE **THE TOOLS THEY NEED TO DO THEIR** JOBS SUCCESSFULLY

I can't begin to count the number of times I've worked with companies, who would hire an employee, give him or her a job description, briefly discuss the job with him or her, and then sit them at a desk or work station and expect them to perform the job satisfactorily. Employees often tell me that they had to figure out how to do their jobs to the best of their ability. It is common for employees to complain that, as new hires, when they posed questions to coworkers, the co-workers would tell them, "I had to learn it on my own, so you have to learn it on your own." This process and behavior is a "new hire set-up for failure."

The Mistake: Although the situation above is a common occurrence, it is a costly mistake due to turnover, which could lead to overtime, overworked staff, low morale (from being overworked), low productivity, and stress.

How to Fix the Mistake: As we discussed in a prior chapter, a detailed orientation, onboarding program, and assigned buddy can really help a new hire become acclimated to the organization and set them up for success. Another positive thing to do is have current employees compose procedural manuals for each job. If the employees are not able to write their own procedural manual, HR or management could be assigned to help them.

What is a procedural manual?
A procedural manual is a written document that lists job instructions, step-by-step instructions on how to complete job tasks and handle specific situations when they arise in the workplace. It can

be an extremely valuable asset as it is a reference for new hires and to the organization. The procedural manual should offer an overview of steps to complete job duties and tasks efficiently, which can facilitate job accomplishment success and enable optimal employee retention. Following the procedural manual can ensure job consistency.

For example: If we were writing a procedural manual for a Receptionist job, the procedural manual may include steps regarding:

- How to handle basic operations or tasks.
- List of information/resources that the employee would refer to on a regular basis; i.e. websites, shared drives, books, etc.
- List the events, board meeting dates, recurring committee meetings, etc.
- List the tools used on the job, i.e., phone, computer, video, microphones, etc.
- List the types of checklists, forms, or templates that are required or that may be helpful.
- Include how to work with others to accomplish tasks.
- Identify top areas/tasks that take the most time investment.
- Who to contact if the media arrives unannounced.
- How to handle irate customers.

When I advise clients to provide this manual to new hires, the success rate increases considerably. This tool can save the organization money, reduce new hire frustration, and promote job consistency.

Mistake

022 | POSSESSING INAPPROPRIATE
PERSONNEL FILES

Okay, I have seen almost everything in personnel files, including a note stating, "Your Mom called, dinner is at 6." I've also seen I-9 forms, medical information, arrest records, investigation reports, the wrong employee's information, etc. All of these things are inappropriate.

The Mistake: The personnel file can be used as evidence in a lawsuit brought on by disgruntled employees. Therefore, it is crucial to know what to include in an employee's file, as well as, what not to include.

If an organization is audited by a government agency, inappropriate information are red flags to the auditor, who may relay the information to other government agencies, who may want to audit your organization as well. Therefore, certain confidential information should not be accessible to other employees or managers who review the file. Staff should only be allowed to review personnel files on a 'need to know' basis.

How to Fix the Mistake: It is essential to maintain an employee file on each employee from the first date of employment to ensure:

- Accurate information is accessible and organized when needed/required.
- You are prepared when encountered with the need for documentation regarding employee performance and/or work history.
- Federal and state requirements.

TYPICALLY THE ITEMS BELOW ARE KEPT IN THE PERSONNEL FILE

Job Application	Performance Evaluations
Interview Evaluation Forms	Complaints from Customers, Co-workers, etc.
Job Offer Letter	Awards, customer compliments, achievements
Job Description	Vacation Forms
Acknowledgement of Acceptance of Employee Manual	Training History Forms
In Case of Emergency Forms	Disciplinary Action Forms, Warnings, Memos, etc.

DON'T INCLUDE THE FOLLOWING IN THE EMPLOYEE FILE

Medical Records, i.e. FMLA information, disability or workers compensation (keep in a separate file and limit access to only a few people)	Forms
Investigation notes and reports	Drug screen records
Arrest records/criminal history	Unnecessary material

Please note: Don't put anything in a personnel file that you would not want a jury to see.

023 | I-9 FORMS INCOMPLETE OR NOT COMPLETED APPROPRIATELY

I can count on one hand the number of times I've seen I-9 Forms completed correctly; and I have seen thousands of them. It is unfortunate that many employers don't utilize the I-9 Form, or follow the law at all, and its also unfortunate that employers don't take the I-9 seriously.

One company never bothered to deal with the forms and when I inquired about it, the HR Representative told me that no one ever paid it any attention anyway. His words exactly were: "I have not seen or heard one government agent ask me about those forms. It is a waste of time and space."

Not a good idea...

The Mistake: U.S. law requires companies to employ only individuals who are legally authorized to work in the United States – either U.S. citizens, or foreign citizens who have the necessary authorization. The Immigration Reform and Control Act (IRCA) of 1986 requires all U.S. employers to verify the identity and employment eligibility of all new employees (both citizen and noncitizen) hired after November 6, 1986. Every employee hired since 1986 must have a completed I-9 Form on file, within 3 days of hire.

In an audit (and we never know when we will be audited), federal agents review the I-9 Form that employers are required to keep on file. The law provides for penalties from $100 to $1,000 for each incorrect or missing I-9. Recently, the government required 1,000 companies to turn over employment records for inspection. Organizations including, Chipotle Mexican Grill, Gebbers Farm, Abercrombie & Fitch received substantial fines for I-9 violations. Disneyland in California was accused of having more than 1,000 paperwork violations and received a $395,000 fine. (Mondy and Martocchio).

It is a huge mistake for employers to request employment verification only for individuals of a particular national origin, or individuals who appear to be or sound foreign, which violates both Title VII and IRCA. Verification must be obtained from all applicants and employees. Employers who impose citizenship requirements or give preferences to U.S. citizens in hiring or employment opportunities also may violate IRCA.

If an employer does not require I-9 Forms or repeatedly makes the same mistake on I-9 Forms; fines and penalties can add up and become excessive for the organization.

How to Fix the Mistake: The obvious way to fix the mistake is for employers to make sure to administer I-9 Forms to each new employee and to make sure they are completed correctly. Employers should avoid the most common errors below:

- Name in wrong order
- Address incomplete
- Social security number field blank (required for employees working on contract with FAR E-Verify clause.)
- Attestation box not checked or is incomplete
- Signature missing
- Date missing
- Date of birth instead of current date
- Employee supplies photocopied or expired proof

Missing I-9 Forms

If an employer discovers a missing I-9 Form, the employer and employee must complete a new I-9 Form. The newly completed form should not be back-dated. If the employee cannot produce acceptable documentation or refuses to complete Section 1 of the I-9 Form, he or she cannot work for pay.

E-Verify

An additional level of verification involves the use of E-Verify to check out new hires, and its use is required for Federal contractors and subcontractors with contracts of $100,000 or more. E-Verify is a web-based system that lets employers check Social Security and Visa numbers submitted by workers against government databases. **The system does not check for citizenship, but for eligibility to be lawfully employed in the United States.** (Mondy and Martocchio)

024 | ALLOWING HOURLY **EMPLOYEES** TO WORK WHILE ON UNPAID LUNCH BREAK

I realize that oftentimes employees may want to work during their unpaid lunch breaks. Employees will say, "I don't mind working during my lunch hour," or, "I have a lot of work to do today, so I will keep working and eat at my desk." I know this happens, because I have observed it several times with my clients, and have even dealt with it with my own staff. In fact, one of my employees, Jimmy, insisted on wanting to work during his unpaid lunch hour. I had to require that he leave during that time. It is also good for the employee to get away from their work area, if possible, and have lunch; then come back refreshed.

The Mistake: Per the United States Department of Labor, bona-fide meal periods (typically 30 minutes or more) are not work time, and an employer does not have to pay for them. However, the employees must be completely relieved from duty. When choosing to automatically deduct 30-minutes per shift, the employer must ensure that the employees are receiving the full meal break.

In 2008, Wal-mart Stores settled a break time suit for $54 million, in part for not stopping managers from cutting worker break time and "willfully" not stopping managers from having employees work off the clock. This is a wakeup call for other employers.

Dedicated hourly employees who insist on working through their lunch hours can become disgruntled employees who report this activity to the government officials, which can incite an investigation. Therefore, allowing hourly employees to work through their unpaid lunch break is a violation of the Fair Labor Standards Act; which can be costly to the employer via fines and penalties for non-compliance.

How to Fix the Mistake: The United States Department Of Labor cites the following examples:

- A skilled nursing facility automatically deducts one-half hour for meal breaks each shift. Upon hiring, the employer notifies employees of the policy and of their responsibility to take a meal break. Does this practice comply with the FLSA? Yes, but **the employer is still responsible for ensuring that the employees take the 30-minute meal break without interruption.**
- An hourly paid registered nurse works at a nursing home, which allows a 30-minute meal break. Residents frequently interrupt her meal break with requests for assistance. Must she be paid for these frequently interrupted meal breaks? Yes, **if employees' meals are interrupted to the extent that meal period is predominately for the benefit of the employer, the employees should be paid for the full 30-minutes.**

It is crucial that employers keep track of hourly employees' lunch breaks. Employers should have policies regarding this issue and the policies should be communicated to hourly employees. Managers and supervisors should be trained to monitor unpaid hourly employee lunch breaks. If employees refuse to stop working during unpaid lunch hours, the disciplinary action process may need to be considered.

Please note: This issue is in regards to unpaid lunch breaks, not short breaks of 5 - 20 minutes long.

025 FAILURE
TO GIVE POSITIVE,
CONSTRUCTIVE
FEEDBACK TO EMPLOYEES

Managers and supervisors typically do a good job when they are out on the floor monitoring employees' production and behavior. In many instances they are very thorough and address poor behavior and performance issues as needed. However, it is rare that the managers and supervisors stop to provide positive, constructive feedback to the employees.

Just take a minute and think about how you felt when someone gave you a compliment; or told you that you did a great job on a project. Remember how you felt? It probably felt great and inspired you to do more bigger and better things. Well, it's the same for the employees. Typically, when you praise them for their good work and provide positive feedback; employees will thrive. When you combine positive, constructive criticism with other feedback it goes over very well for employees.

The Mistake: Assuming employees know what they are doing well or waiting to praise employees during the performance evaluation is a mistake. If employees are not receiving feedback, it may be construed as management not caring about their work; which, in turn, could cause morale issues, then production issues, and on and on...

How to Fix the Mistake: Take the time to praise employees for jobs well done. If they provide outstanding customer service to a client, let them know you appreciate their efforts. If you receive positive feedback about your employee, let them know immediately. Organizations that stroke their employees and treat them well, are generally profitable.

026 | FAILURE
TO ADMINISTER
PERFORMANCE
EVALUATIONS ON EMPLOYEES

During an HR Audit, "Simon," the Facilities Coordinator, requested to speak with me. Simon told me a story I will never forget.

This is Simon's Story: "I was promoted to the Director of Facilities a year ago. I was excited and really loved it, I did my best. I stayed late and came in early. I had been in the position for about nine (9) months, and while out to lunch one day, I received a phone call from the Vice-President. The VP apologized that he unable to speak to me in person that day; so, he said he left a note on my desk. The VP did not give any details about the contents of the note; therefore I rushed back to the office, speculating and thinking about the contents of the note. Upon my return, I hurriedly read the note, which said I was not a good fit for the job and not a good Director. The note further stated I was being demoted back to the Facilities Coordinator position, effective immediately. My heart dropped and I immediately went to look for the VP to get some clarification and understanding as to why I was being demoted. Unfortunately, the VP had left for the day."

I asked Simon if he had received an evaluation during the 9 months he was in the position and he said, "No, nobody ever said a thing, I did not receive an evaluation or any feedback; I thought I was doing a great job. I am still not sure what I did wrong."

So, how would you feel?... Most of us, exactly like Simon!

The Mistake: As the above scenario outlines, when employees do not receive feedback and/or evaluations it is difficult, if not impossible, for the employee to understand company expectations. The employee may feel they are doing their jobs correctly and may believe they are exceeding expectations. In essence, they could be failing. I ask you this, what type of atmosphere will be created if employees are confused as to their expectations. It could devastating to productivity.

How To Fix the Mistake: Employers should take the time to conduct performance evaluation. It is recommended that new hires be evaluated every 30 days, 60 days and 90 days. Regular employees should be evaluated bi-annually at the least. Promoted employees should be evaluated the same as a new hire.

Providing evaluations take the guesswork out of employee performance and expectations.

Mistake

027 | USING THE SAME METHOD AND
TECHNIQUE
TO MANAGE AND/OR
SUPERVISE ALL EMPLOYEES

It's easy to think of all employees the same, and to manage them the same, and keep them all in a little box; right? No, wrong. Each employee is different. Employees have different walks of life, are different ages, races, cultures, etc. Therefore, everyone does not understand things the same way.

For example, at one time, my staff included millennials and baby boomers. In one case, the millennial required much more direction, feedback, and praise than the baby boomer. The baby boomer just wanted me to give her the work assignment and leave her to get it done. She didn't need constant praise or continuous direction.

A good manager takes the time to get to know their employees and the employees' specific needs. I know it takes a lot of time and work, but it will be well worth it when your morale is up, profits are up, and your headaches are down.

The Mistake: The mistake is having across the board managing and not being in tune to your employees' needs to succeed in their individual positions. Per the example above, it you treated the baby boomer the same as the millennial, the baby boomer may get angry and feel you don't trust her. If it was the other way around, the millennial may fell ignored and neglected. This could cause a lag in productivity.

How to Fix the Mistake: Make sure managers are trained on how to communicate and manage the different generations, cultures, genders, etc. The chart below is a sample of generational characteristics.

TYPICAL GENERATIONAL CHARACTERISTICS

Traditionalists Born before 1946	Baby Boomers Born 1946 to 1965	Generation X Born 1966 to 1980	Millenials, aka Generation Y Born 1981 to 2000
Characteristics: • Loyal • Patriotic • Legacy minded • Fiscally conservative • Strong faith/ belief in institutions	Characteristics: • Strong work ethic • Respect for hierarchy • Goal driven • Believe in "face time" • Value Consensus	Characteristics: • Independent minded • Self reliant • Skeptical of institutions/ authorities • Value work/ life balance and freedom to work	Characteristics: • Optimistic • Sociable • Demand Flexible work • Techno savvy & connected 24/7 • Environment minded
Defining Technology in their era: Radio	Defining Technology in their era: Television	Defining Technology in their era: Personal Computer	Defining Technology in their era: Internet
Defining moments: Great depression, Pearl Harbor, WWII	Defining moments: Civil Rights Movement, Vietnam War, Cold War	Defining moments: Berlin Wall, Recession, corporate downsizing	Defining moments: Global economy, Pocket IT, Iraq War, Enron

028 | NOT RECOGNIZING THAT EMPLOYEES ARE YOUR GREATEST ASSETS

In 2009, my company was very new; however, I received a call from an associate, Rick, who stated, "Go over to Andy's Place, he needs your help." As a new business owner, I was eager to see as many potential clients as possible, so I headed right over to "Andy's Place," which was a large restaurant. I remember the meeting well. I conversed with Andy for the first 5 minutes, over the counter, and at first Andy said, "I don't think I need this service."

After a little more discussion, Andy and I moved from the counter, to a booth; there we talked for 3 more hours! I found out that Andy had big problems with his company; he had 4 locations and only frequented one of them. During our 3-hour conversation, Andy told me that his revenue had dropped and he was having multiple issues. One of the questions I asked him was had he spoken to his employees. He said "No!" and looked at me as if that was out of the question. I asked him if I could conduct an HR audit and do a review of his restaurants, which included speaking to his managers and pertinent employees. He agreed; and we entered into our first of many contracts...

To make a long story short, I interviewed many of Andy's employees at all of the locations. Some of them had outstanding ideas that could really add to the bottom line. For example, one employee stated he tried out a new dish in the restaurant; he stated it was very popular and sold out each of the four times he provided the dish. He stated customers loved it and kept asking for the dish. He said he was excited about the popularity of the dish so he mentioned putting it on the menu to management, but, he said, nobody cared. The employee appeared to feel defeated; he was a cook and his ideas were ignored.

I brought many of the employees' ideas back to Andy along with many other issues that needed to be addressed. Issues such as: Compliance, policies, streamlining processes, etc. Together, Andy and I actually implemented several of the ideas, including adding the cook's dish, at all locations, and naming it after the cook. Andy's revenue grew! We continued to work together over time. Andy's revenue was increasing at a commendable pace, he was becoming profitable again and, boy was he happy. Unfortunately, in 2015, Andy passed away. I sincerely miss Andy.

The Mistake: Not listening to employees. I have interviewed hundreds of employees; in most instances while conducting HR Audits. It is amazing how employees can help with the strategy of the organization and often aid in improving the bottom line. In most instances, employees are on the front lines. They know the problems; they know what works and what does not work. Employees know how to make the job more efficient and often they know how to make the business profitable. Ignoring them and thinking they are just there to go through the motions of job tasks, can be a huge mistake.

How to Fix the Mistake: Maintain an organization that is inclusive of everyone's thoughts and ideas. Conduct annual employee surveys and HR Audits. LISTEN to your employees. Not all comments will lead to an idea, but you will be super surprised in the process and of efficiency improvements you will be alerted to by employees. There is nothing wrong with listening and learning from your subordinates. It can pay handsomely!

Mistake

| ## LACK OF CONSISTENCY AMONG
MANAGERS
AND SUPERVISORS

At one point, I worked with an organization that had 10 locations. Unfortunately, the managers at each of those locations were on different pages. For instance, if an employee was late at Location A, the manager would discipline them. However if an employee was late at Location B, the Manager would tell the employee to not be late again. So, the employee at Location A could progress by disciplinary action and get terminated, whereas the employee at Location B might be employed forever, without incident.

The Mistake: Regarding the above example, how long do you think it will take for employees to talk among themselves about the process? Not long. Imagine what this process does to morale. Eventually, the employees at Location A may become disgruntled and claim discrimination. You probably understand where this is going...

How to Fix the Mistake: It is crucial that mangers and supervisor are on the same page when it comes to managing employees within the organization. Conduct rules and discipline should be as consistent as possible. It is acknowledged that some violations or issues may be a little different and some issue have just a little different "spin" to them; if this happens, the reason for the variance should be acceptable and well-documented.

030 | NOT REFERENCING THE **EMPLOYEE HANDBOOK AND/OR UNION CONTRACTS WHEN** MAKING DECISIONS

Typically, I see this mistake more so with new HR professionals and managers. The issue could be as small as an employee is an hour late. What should the manager do? Sometimes the manager will quickly give the employee a "write-up" or disciplinary action; without checking the employee handbook or union contract to make sure the action is in compliance with the union contract and/ or consistent with the employee handbook.

The Mistake: Employee Handbooks are not contracts and are intended to communicate expectations of employees and what employees can expect of the organization. However, when managers deviate from the handbook, it can cause implications of discrimination, unfairness, and/or favoritism. These inferences can lead to disgruntled employees, which can lead to costly unnecessary litigation.

Union Contracts are legal documents that result from negotiations with company management and the union. They include specific employee rights, benefits, and most times wages. When the union contract is ignored, the organization could suffer unfair labor practices, have to deal with time-consuming grievances and arbitrations, or endure expensive lawsuits.

How to Fix the Mistake: Managers, supervisor, coordinators, etc. (as appropriate) should be trained in the process of handling employee wrongdoing or performance issues; especially newly hired management. I recommend having them read both the handbook and union contract, cover to cover, before they begin working with employees and annually. It is also important that the management team interpret the handbook and contract consistently. It is a good idea to have someone on the management team to take minutes during union negotiations to act a resource when language in the union contract is questionable regarding its meaning.

Mistake

031 | NOT DOCUMENTING EMPLOYEE ISSUES APPROPRIATELY

Document, document, document! When providing HR consulting I use these three words over and over again; from client to client, almost daily. However, it never fails, most employers just wont do it. They will not take the time to document. Why? After almost 20 years in HR, I am still trying to figure that one out.

In my early days as a new business owner, I worked with a client named Jane. She had a very small company, about 20 employees, and had been in business about two years. Jane became a member of my company, Expert Human Resources. I composed Jane's handbook and explained to her the importance of following the handbook as much as possible and to always document issues, even if it is just documentation for herself; in case she may need it in the future. Jane stated she understood.

About three months later, Jane called me. She said she received an unemployment document in the mail requesting information about Kelvin, whom she fired. She asked me how she should respond.

First of all, I was surprised she fired Kelvin without calling me because she was a member of the company. So I asked her which rule did

Kelvin violate. She stated that Kelvin had violated the rules three times, and she went on to list them all, i.e. he was late, he was rude to a customer, and the last straw was he stole money from petty cash. I asked her if she could gather her documentation and I could review everything. Jane said, "I didn't write any documentation; I just fired him on the spot."

No documentation. No call to me. Bad move.

The Mistake: Documentation is evidence when faced with litigation or charges of unfair labor practices. Not having documentation or adequate documentation can be the determining factor to cause employers to lose in court.

How To Fix the Mistake: Managers and Supervisors should get in the habit of documenting frequently for various issues, including:

- Violation of company policies, rules, management direction
- Coaching and counseling
- Recurring incidents
- Negative change in work performance, work quality, quantity of work
- Performance management, terminations, complaints
- Sample Issues to document include:
- Drinking on the job
- Employee disputes
- Using phone or internet for personal business
- Rude to co-workers, customers
- Excessive unscheduled absences or tardiness
- Performance issues, i.e. lack of detail, slow performance, missing assignments, careless workmanship
- Customer complaints
- Inappropriate dress
- Careless workmanship
- Safety rule violations
- Using profanity
- Bullying and/or harassment

Remember: Appropriate documentation can be the difference of winning or losing when faced with costly litigation.

Mistake

032 | EMPLOYEE
BEHAVIOR IN THE WORKPLACE

As part of a third party investigation, I had to inform an accused employee, Curtis, that there had been complaints filed against him. The complaint involved five (5) female employees. Curtis became extremely upset and irate about the complaints. Although the complaints did not appear to lead to suspension or termination, he was outraged. He was given the policies regarding the violation and retaliation, with a heavy warning to refrain from retaliating against his accusers.

After completing the investigation, which was substantiated, Curtis was issued a written warning. He became angrier. My thoughts, "we have a problem here." The employer felt that Curtis would get over the anger and would be fine. I advised the employer on how best to handle Curtis, additionally, recommended that he consult with Curtis and closely monitor his actions. The employer did not monitor nor follow-through and Curtis' attitude got worse, and he retaliated.

The Mistake: Workplace violence is on the rise. The Occupational Safety and Health Administration (OSHA) requires that employers provide their employees with safe and healthful workplaces. OSHA further requires that employers have a due diligence responsibility of taking at least reasonable precautions to provide a healthy and safe work environment. Employers who do not take reasonable steps to prevent violence in the workplace can be cited.

How to Fix the Mistake: It is crucial that employers constantly monitor the workplace and note any abnormal or violent behavior. Extreme anger can turn into violence. Employers should be aware of how to spot a potentially violent person in the workplace.

The Department of Labor publishes on their website how to recognize levels of potential or actual violence, which includes:

1. **Level One (Early Warning Signs) – The person is:**
   - Intimidating/bullying;
   - Discourteous/disrespectful;
   - Uncooperative; and/or
   - Verbally abusive.

2. **Level Two (Escalation of the Situation) – The person:**
   - Argues with customers, vendors, co-workers, and management;
   - Refuses to obey agency policies and procedures;
   - Sabotages equipment and steals property for revenge;
   - Verbalizes wishes to hurt co-workers and/or management;
   - Sends threatening note(s) to co-worker(s) and/or management; and/or
   - Sees self as victimized by management (me against them).

In the story listed above, Curtis saw himself as the victim, which could be an escalation (Level Two above). As I am not a psychologist and am merely giving suggestions in this book; I would advise that if you observe these signs in your employee, take prompt action, report it, and seek assistance right away.

Mistake

033 | IMPROPER AND/OR DISCRIMINATORY PAY PRACTICES

Although this is the 21st century, two years ago I found myself listening to an employer explain why he paid a male employee more than he paid a female employee to perform the same job duties. "He has 3 kids and is going thru a nasty divorce." The employer continued with his explanation with "It's costing him a lot of money and his wife didn't work, so he will probably have to pay alimony." I could not believe my ears. In many cases gender pay discrepancies are errors in judgment or just mistakes. In this case, I was listening to someone who either was not aware of the Equal Pay Act, which had been around forever, or he just didn't care what the law required.

After getting over my disbelief, I presented the law to him as well as the consequences of not following the law. Now, back to the 21st century...

The Mistake: The Equal Pay Act of 1963 prohibits paying lower wages to one sex than the other sex for similar jobs. Oftentimes employers believe their pay system is fair if they pay different salaries to different genders if the job titles are different. However, the Equal Pay Act of 1963 states job titles are not the determining factor.

How to Fix the Mistake: It is crucial that employers review their job descriptions and pay practices. The Equal Pay Act prohibits paying lower wages to one sex than the other sex for jobs that are similar in terms of:

- Job tasks
- Skill
- Effort
- Responsibility
- Working Conditions

However, differentials in compensation are allowed for seniority systems, merit systems, system based on quantity or quality of production and any other factors other than sex. Additionally, the Act does not include benefits.

034 | NEGLIGENTLY RETAINING **EMPLOYEES** WHO SHOULD BE TERMINATED

Joyce, Office Manager of a health care organization, complained about an employee, Jerry. According to Joyce, Jerry was aggressive towards a Doctor. Jerry's aggressive behavior included getting in the doctor's face, yelling at him, used profanity, and displayed a high-level of anger towards him. Joyce further reported that Jerry then went down the corridor yelling at his co-workers.

That's a lot! But then there's more.

Jerry ran down the corridor twice (running is prohibited). Joyce told me that when she talked to Jerry, he yelled at her and told her he was tired of the B***S*** at the company and things had better change. She said Jerry was so angry and loud that she sent him home. I expressed to Joyce that the issue was extremely concerning, and based on Jerry's violent behavior, as well as other pertinent information, I recommended termination. Unfortunately, Joyce did not act on my recommendation.

Three months later, Joyce called again complaining about Jerry. He had again yelled at the doctor, his coworkers, and was using profanity. Jerry had not been terminated three months ago because the doctor didn't want to try to find another person on such short notice.

Oh boy...

The Mistake: Not taking immediate action regarding Jerry, Joyce now runs the risk of Jerry creating an unsafe and unhealthy work environment. **The Occupational Safety and Health Administration** (OSHA) defines workplace violence as any act or threat of physical violence, harassment, intimidation, or other threatening disruptive behavior that occurs at the work site. It ranges from threats and verbal abuse to physical assaults and even homicide. Further, OSHA law requires that employers provide safe and healthful workplaces for employees. Violating OSHA requirements can cause detrimental consequences, i.e. fines, penalties. Some offences can lead to imprisonment.

How to Fix the Mistake: Per OSHA, *in most workplaces where risk factors can be identified, the risk of assault can be prevented or minimized if employers take appropriate precautions. One of the best protections employers can offer their workers is to establish a zero-tolerance policy toward workplace violence. This policy should cover all workers, customers, clients, visitors, contractors, and anyone else who may come in contact with company personnel.*

It is also a good idea to train managers and supervisors regarding OSHA requirements, as well as appropriate discipline and termination procedures.

Mistake

035 | TOLERATING AN EMPLOYEE'S POOR PERFORMANCE

It is not uncommon for employers to say things like:

- "John is late all of the time, and has been consistently late for years"; or
- "Jane's work performance has been unsatisfactory for years"; or
- "Katie was never a good employee. And she bullies the other staff"; or
- "Sam hired in with a bad attitude and its getting worse"; or
- "Amanda is always rude and disrespectful to customers"; or
- "Holly does not work well with the team and continually distracts other employees with her constant phone calls and drama";

When I ask why the employer tolerates this behavior, the answer is almost always, "I've talked to him/her about it a few times and thought it would get better."

The Mistake: Poor performers can drain the organization. Not addressing poor performance causes reduced productivity, which can lead to reduced profits. Typically other employees have to work harder to cover the slack of the poor performing employee. This can lead to low morale. Additionally, the co-workers of the poor performer may become disgruntled, and when the employer does not address poor performance, the co-worker may believe it is due to favoritism or discrimination.

How to Fix the Mistake: Employers should address poor performers and be prepared to demote, discipline or terminate as needed. Employers should ensure that poor performers know what is expected of them and make sure that they have the tools they need to perform their jobs appropriately. Also, Performance Improvement Plans could be used as needed to keep track of and list the following:

- The performance issue(s),
- Employee responsibilities,
- Performance expectation(s) for improvement,
- Actions employee will take to aid improvements,
- Actions employer will take to aid improvements,
- A timeline for improvement,
- Progress reviews and comments, and
- Employer responsibilities, i.e., meetings between the employer and employee.

If the poor performer does not improve after performing the above, termination may need to occur. Remember, poor performers can hurt the organization in more ways than performance.

036 | I G N O R I N G
HARASSMENT
C O M P L A I N T S

A few years back, as part of an HR audit, I interviewed an employee named Cindy. Cindy seemed a little reserved and gave me a look like "what can you do about this place." I've seen that look so many times that I can recognize it right away. I went through the list of questions with Cindy and then asked her if she had any questions or comments. She quietly told me about a male employee, Marvin, who she stated, had been constantly bothering her and it was causing her to be stressed. She said he came on her job site 2 or 3 times a day, put breakfast bars and candies on her work table almost every day, left her notes on her car, and was just being a constant nuisance.

I asked her had she reported it to her supervisor. She answered "yes" and had gone so far as to complain to two (2) managers. She further stated that she was told that Marvin was probably a little infatuated with her but they felt Marvin was completely harmless. She said she was basically told his behavior would run its course and take care of itself.

Later, it was discovered that Cindy had suffered with Marvin's inappropriate behavior for almost two (2) years. This was a huge issue.

The Mistake: Not addressing Cindy's complaint can cause her to work in a hostile work environment, which can also be harassment. Per the EEOC, below is the legal definition of hostile work environment:

A hostile work environment ensues when there is discriminatory conduct or behavior in the place of work that is unwelcome and offensive to an employee or group of employees based on a protected class status.

What does this mean? In litigation, the complainant must be a member of a protected class under that state's law (women, disabled, and a specific race) and the complaint should pertain directly to perceived discrimination that specifically targets that class.

It is extremely important to make sure the "hostile work environment" is not harassment. **A claim of harassment can be very expensive to the organization as well as distracting to the workforce.**

According to the EEOC, the legal definition of harassment is: *Unwelcome conduct that is based on race, color, religion, sex (including pregnancy), national origin, age (40 or older), disability or genetic information. Harassment becomes unlawful where 1) enduring the offensive conduct becomes a condition of continued employment, or 2) the conduct is severe or pervasive enough to create a work environment that a reasonable person would consider intimidating, hostile, or abusive.*

And regarding the harasser: *The harasser can be the victim's supervisor, a supervisor in another area, and an agent of the employer, a co-worker, or a non-employee. The victim does not have to be the person harassed, but can be anyone affected by the offensive conduct.*

How to Fix the Mistake: Employers should take formal and informal complains of harassment seriously; and should investigate those complaints promptly. Employers should also make sure to conduct annual Anti-Harassment training for management and for all employees. Anti-Harassment training can be added to orientation to ensure all new hires have this information when they begin employment.

037 | ADMINISTERING
DISCIPLINE THAT DOES NOT
FIT THE VIOLATION

Alberta was employed by a large non-profit organization. Alberta wanted to know why the VP of Facilities had not been at work for 2 weeks. She felt senior management was keeping it a secret. Every time she asked why he was not at work, they told her, "He is on leave." Of course, this was not enough information for Alberta; she wanted to know the details so badly that she was distressed about the whole thing. Alberta decided to ignore employee confidentiality and HIPAA rules; she accessed the VP's information via the company's computer to find out why the VP was off work. Alberta found out that the VP had a serious disease. Then she was satisfied.

What Alberta didn't know was that the organization conducted regular audits of computer access. Management determined that Alberta accessed the VP's information without a reason to do so. Since her manager liked her, Alberta received a verbal discipline for her actions.

Nine months later, Alberta's manager was summoned to his boss' office. After the meeting, her manager looked very upset. Alberta wanted to know what was going on, but she did not want to get in trouble again. So Albert decided to wait until her co-worker left his computer and she quickly used his computer to access the manager's information. She found out that the manager made a huge mistake and had been reprimanded.

After an investigation of the co-workers' access of the managers' information, it was determined that Alberta was the culprit.

The Mistake: In 1996, The Health Insurance Portability and Accountability Act (HIPAA) was signed into law. The intent behind the HIPPA law is to protect the privacy of every medical record and strengthens every individual's control of personal health records by giving greater control of its use and disclosure.

Alberta's first offense could be a HIPAA violation. It is the Employers duty to ensure penalties for violations are appropriate. Specifically, the employer's duty, once triggered by a reasonable suspicion that a problem might exist, is two-fold: (1) reasonable investigation and, based on the findings, (2) reasonable intervention. Reasonable intervention, in negligent retention cases, typically amounts to taking the appropriate actions to prevent reoccurrence of the offense. So you ask yourself, was the action appropriate to prevent reoccurrence? I think not.

Additionally, penalties for non-compliance with the HIPPA law are serious and hefty. Based on the level of negligence determined, they can be as much as $50,000 per violation (or record), up to a maximum of $1.5 million per year for repeat violations.

How to Fix the Mistake: When dealing with disciplines, it is a good idea for employers to contract and consult with an HR guru/consultant to ensure disciplines are appropriate for the violation. The HR guru may be able to give advice regarding the discipline as well when to involve legal counsel. Also, employers should make sure managers are trained and understand how to administer disciplinary action properly.

038 | MISHANDLING INVESTIGATION DECISIONS

Last year, I found myself conducting a third party investigation for a midsize manufacturing company. The investigation involved the COO and 4 female complainants. The complainants stated the COO had touched them inappropriately, yelled at them in front of other co-workers, insulted them, and used profanity towards them. This was surprising to me, as the COO seemed to carry himself respectfully, was friendly, and appeared to be admired by the management team.

The investigation uncovered email evidence and witnesses who verified the accusations of the complainants. The investigation report verified the complaints; the allegations were substantiated.

Due to the seriousness of the COO's behavior, and based on the law; one of our recommendations was disciplinary action, appropriate for the offense. We met with and provided the CEO, Stephanie, with the results of the investigation. We reviewed the evidence with Stephanie. Feeling really confident that she would take immediate action; Stephanie stated, "Do you know what a charge like this can do to his (COO's) reputation?" She further commented, "We've worked hard to get into these positions and it would be unfair to let a charge like this damage his character." Stephanie refused to take action.

I was taken aback...

The Mistake: Mishandling substantiated investigation reports can set the company up for expensive litigation. Per the EEOC, an employer is subject to vicarious liability for unlawful harassment if the harassment was committed by "a supervisor with immediate (or successively higher) authority over the employee. The employer may be able to limit liability if it can show that it was aware of the harassment and had taken immediate, appropriate corrective action."

How to Fix the Mistake: Employers should conduct prompt investigations for all complaints, formal or informal; even if the employee is a complainer. Investigative reports/documentation should be written and kept. It is important to have a Director or upper management review your report or to contract with an HR Guru/Consultant to review the report. If there is a relationship between the investigator and the accused or complainant, consider a third party investigator to help protect the company from lawsuits.

After an investigation, the employer should take immediate and appropriate corrective action by doing whatever is necessary to end the harassment and prevent the harassment from reoccurring. Substantiated allegations should lead to corrective action as appropriate for the offender, even if it is a supervisor or senior leader. Additionally, the penalty should fit the violation. Employers should also work to make the victim of the harassment whole by restoring any lost pay, benefits, etc. The complainant should never be treated negatively or retaliated against for his or her allegations. If the complainant's accusation is deliberately false, it should be dealt with per the employer's False Claims Policy and disciplinary process.

Employers, please remember, all complaints must be taken seriously, and appropriate action should be taken. All managers, supervisors and other designated individuals should be trained to react appropriately and promptly to any complaints.

039 | L A C K   O F COMMUNICATION TO EMPLOYEES

As a result of conducting multiple HR Audits and interviewing numerous employees, I would estimate that about 98% of employees tell me there is a lack of communication at their organization. Approximately 90% of them share that it's company wide. It's very common for me to hear the following:

- "I was working on my job as I usually do and was told I was processing 'the widget' wrong; but no one told me the process had changed."
- "Management changed my job and did not even talk to me about it first. Now I have to do more steps to get my job done, which takes me more time. I could have shown them if they had given me the chance."
- "I feel like my input is not important. They don't care."
- "Management sneaks around and discusses things among themselves. They don't talk to us. Its like they have a private club."
- "There is a quicker, better way to do this, but management doesn't want to hear it."
- "We never know a change is coming until the last minute, then we have to work long hours to get it done."
- "My supervisor will tell me to do one thing and then his boss, the Director will come in and tell me to do something else."
- "They (management) make changes and never talk to us. We are treated like machines instead of people."

The Mistake: Lack of communicating appropriately with employees can cause:

- Negativity and low morale,

- Decreased employee engagement,
- Increased rumor mill,
- Low motivation and productivity, which can lead to
- Reduced revenue and profits

How to Fix the Mistake: Proper communication to employees is extremely important to the success of the organization. It can cause employees to be engaged. Communication can be achieved via frequent staff meetings, the intranet, emails (if the employees have access to email), memos, conference calls, Skype, etc.

Additionally, engaged employees are more productive, which can encourage them to go above and beyond for the company. Also, employees can give ideas to help the company be more profitable; as they typically are on the front lines and know the product or service very well.

Mistake

040 | FLUFFING THE PERFORMANCE EVALUATION

Harvey, Director of Finance, followed the rules and evaluated his staff annually. Harvey's employee, Barbara, was an okay worker, but she struggled to get her work done and did not complete it most of the time. Her attendance was not too good, but she took Harvey his coffee everyday, kept the kitchen area clean, got along with co-workers, and smiled a lot.

When the time arrived to complete Barbara's performance evaluation, Harvey decided to give Barbara all outstanding scores. He believed that if he was honest regarding her performance evaluation, it might prevent her from receiving a promotion in the future. He completed the same process for 5-years; everything was fine.

Due to Barbara's outstanding performance review scores, she was promoted. Her new supervisor, Kirk, was excited and happy to have Barbara as part of his team. After 3 weeks, Kirk noticed that Barbara was falling way behind and couldn't keep up with the demands of the job. Although she brought him coffee every day, she still couldn't keep up. Kirk's team had to meet production expectations. Kirk counseled Barbara and gave her multiple chances to improve; however despite Barbara's best efforts, she was not able to perform the job. After 3 months, Barbara had not improved; as a result, Kirk had no choice but to fire Barbara.

Barbara was very angry about being terminated and obtained a lawyer. She told her attorney that Kirk discriminated against her and then shared all of her outstanding performance evaluations from the past 5-years. She told the attorney that when she went to work for Kirk, he did not like her because she was a woman.

Get the picture...

The Mistake: Not being truthful on the performance evaluation can backfire on organizations. Employees can become disgruntled and use it against the employer. The employer will have to explain why the employee's poor performance was not reflected in the evaluation; therefore not addressed. Fluffing the performance evaluation can be a contributing factor in a long, drawn-out litigation.

How to Fix the Mistake: The best practice is to be as honest as possible in the Employee Performance Evaluation. Being honest will not only help the organization, it will help the employee to improve and grow. Additionally, other employers may rely on your performance evaluations to make hiring and promotional decisions; the same as Kirk relied on Harvey's performance evaluations of Barbara.

I G N O R I N G
041 | RETALIATION
I S S U E S

Think about this scenario. You have a best friend of 20 years. You were his best man at his wedding and you even gave him an expensive wedding gift. He's the Vice-President of Finance at your firm and you even pay him six-figures. You have an extensive history with this friend. Then, one day the inconceivable happens, you find out that your best friend has embezzled over a million dollars from your firm and even stolen your girlfriend. You are now alone and broke.

What if this was your scenario; would you want to retaliate? Most people would, it's human nature.

Well, people in the workplace tend to have the same thought patterns. I have worked with managers who told me that they went above and beyond for their employees, such as, given them the day off and covered for them, because they were short-staffed; some have even given bonuses for staying late; and others have allowed employees to come in late so the employees could handle childcare issues. In one case, the employer permitted an employee to use the company vehicle when the employee's car was being repaired. After all of that "special treatment," one day, that employee files a claim against that manager. The manager is now upset! How dare him!" or, "How dare her!" This is typically how retaliation starts...

The Mistake: Retaliation is the #1 claim filed with the EEOC. Why? Because, when an employee complains about discrimination, harassment, or another charge, it is not uncommon for the employer to retaliate. Subsequently, the employee files a second charge of retaliation. The sad part is the employee may lose the initial claim but win the retaliation claim.

How to Fix the Mistake: When employers receive complaints of harassment, discrimination, etc., it is crucial that employers monitor the workplace to ensure retaliation does not result from the complaint. Oftentimes, managers and supervisors get very upset when complaints are filed against them; and the natural response for many of them is to retaliate against the employee. It can be subtle at first, such as: denying a day off, not answering emails, paying more attention to other employees, ignoring the complainant, delays in responding to the needs of the complainant, etc. When this happens, not only will the employee have the initial complaint, they could file retaliation charges as well.

Senior level management should be aware of complaints filed against managers and supervisors and should make sure that retaliation does not arise, as a result of the complaint, by monitoring the managers and supervisors. If possible, it may be best to move the employee to be supervised under a different manager to avoid retaliation. Additionally, performance reviews should be conduced by the senior manager or alternate manager, while complaints are being investigated.

It is critical that managers and supervisor be trained regarding retaliation.

042 | NOT ADDRESSING
BULLYING
IN THE WORKPLACE

About 4 years ago, while evaluating a company's turnover issue, I met Martha, the Operations Clerk. Martha shared that she would be quitting her job on Friday due to her manager, Roy, whom, she said treated her badly. "He speaks to me like I am a 2-year old. And he yells at me almost every day." I asked her to give examples of Roy's conduct. She stated that Roy would often say to her:

- "You better get this done now!"
- "If you don't like how I manage you and this department, there's the door!"
- "You better be glad you have a job!"
- "What does it take for you to get it?!

She further stated that she was stressed, always fearful of making a mistake, and constantly on the edge. I thanked Martha for her input and assured her I would look into the matter.

Later that day, I met with Justin, Vice-President of the company. Justin was Roy's superior so I shared with Justin the conversation I had with Martha. Justin stated that he knew that Roy could be dominating, however, felt that Roy had the ability "to get the work done and is good for business." He discounted Roy's behavior by stating that "it was just Roy's personality." "Personally," Justin said, "I don't have a problem with him. He has his employees in line and gets work done on time. I just need the employees to stop complaining."

The Mistake: Did you know that bosses are the majority of the bullies in the workplace and that according to **Workplace Bullying**

Institute, 1 in 3 workers (37 million) experience workplace abuse? Also, 20% of workplace bullying crosses the line into harassment; and, 3 out of 4 managers who witness bullying either deny, discount, encourage, rationalize or defend bullying behavior. This is why bullying is referred to as the "silent epidemic."

According to the **Workplace Bullying Institute**, 71% of employees bullied at work had to be treated by a physician for work-related symptoms; and 63% of the victims had to see a mental health professional for their work-related symptoms. The symptoms included: Hypertension, sleeplessness, ulcers, severe mood swings, debilitating anxiety, panic attacks, clinical depression, migraine headaches, relapse of previously controlled addictions, even post traumatic stress disorder. Therefore, bullying can cause an unhealthy workplace and may create a hostile work environment. Allowing this behavior can be costly to the organization in areas such as healthcare benefit costs, absenteeism, low productivity, as well as costly litigation.

How to Fix the Mistake: There is a thin line between assertiveness
in managing employees and bullying employees. Therefore, it is crucial that employers understand and communicate the difference. Let me share with you five (5) things I advise clients to do when dealing with a perceived bully:

1. **Evaluate/assess the situation.**
   Evaluate the situation neutrally. Is this person really a bully or are they having a bad day.

2. **Determine if the person is possessing bullying behaviors. Such as:**
   • Shouting;
   • Name-calling;
   • Belittling, berating, or disrespectful comments;
   • Stealing credit for others' work;
   • Criticizing others;
   • Undermining employees' work;
   • Withholding relevant information;
   • Threatening others;
   • Excluding others from conversations, and/or
   • Making employees feel unwelcome.

3. **Observe how the behavior affects others.** Usually the bully causes workers to become withdrawn, fearful, and/or stressed. The culture is usually affected by the bullying behavior.

4. **Tell the "bully" to stop!** It is a good idea to sit down and have a discussion
    with the perceived bully about the issues, and present pertinent policies to him or her.

5. **Train the bully.** I typically recommend training of the entire staff to ensure everyone is educated in the proper way to conduct themselves as well as how they can expect to be treated in the workplace, i.e., with respect.

If the bullying persists after completing the above steps, unfortunately, you may have to move to disciplinary action up to and including termination. Remember, when you are remiss in dealing with a bully, the problem magnifies which could lead to a huge lawsuit.

Mistake

043 | *IMPROPERLY* **UTILIZING** **UNPAID INTERNS**

Reagan, a very friendly and kind receptionist, quickly greeted me when I arrived to meet with the CEO, Jessica. Reagan graciously escorted me to Jessica's office. I complimented Jessica on her choice of receptionists. "Yes," Jessica said, "she is the best receptionist I have ever had. Reagan is efficient, she answers the phones professionally, handles my calendar, scheduled meetings, takes notes, and a variety of other tasks. And guess what? She is an unpaid intern! I don't have to pay anything for her!"

The Mistake: According to the U.S. Department of Labor, "an unpaid internship is only lawful in the context of an educational training program, when the interns do not perform productive work and the employer derives no benefit. If the employer would have hired additional employees or required existing staff to work additional hours had the interns not performed the work, then the interns will be viewed as employees and entitled to compensation under the FLSA."

Employing unpaid interns can be a good thing as it helps the intern to gain valuable experience about the job(s) at the company. However, using them as an employee can be a violation of the Fair Labor Standards Act, which is an expensive violation. For example, in 2015, Media giant Viacom agreed to pay $7.21 million to settle a class-action lawsuit by thousands of former interns who said the owner of Comedy Central, MTV, and Nickelodeon did not pay them, despite their having done work similar to paid employees. The interns indicated they received no compensation even though they completed tasks—like taking lunch orders, answering phones, and making travel arrangements—that were typically the responsibility of paid employees. (Huffington Post)

How to Fix the Mistake: Employers should ensure that unpaid interns are utilized properly. **The US Department of Labor's Fact Sheet #71: Internship Programs Under the Fair Labor Standards Act** can be a valuable resource for employers. Among other things, the fact sheet lists a test for unpaid interns. Per the fact sheet, the following six (6) criteria must be applied when making unpaid intern determinations:

1. The internship, even though it includes actual operation of the facilities of the employer, is similar to training which would be given in an educational environment;
2. The internship experience is for the benefit of the intern;
3. The intern does not displace regular employees, but works under close supervision of existing staff;
4. The employer that provides the training derives no immediate advantage from the activities of the intern; and on occasion its operations may actually be impeded;
5. The intern is not necessarily entitled to a job at the conclusion of the internship; and
6. The employer and the intern understand that the intern is not entitled to wages for the time spent in the internship.

Therefore, it is a good idea for employers to keep this resource available

Mistake

TERMINATING
044 | EMPLOYEES
WHILE ANGRY

After leaving a meeting, I checked my cellphone and noticed that Danny, Owner of a hospitality company, had called me twice within the last 15 minutes. I quickly called him back. Danny was noticeably upset and was almost yelling on the phone, "Vanessa," he said, "I'm so mad. I can't believe what happened! I am firing Samantha today!" I remained calm while speaking with Danny to try to calm him down. "What happened Danny?" I asked. "I told her I was changing her assignment for tomorrow and she rolled her eyes at me. She is done!" he yelled. I told Danny that I understood his issue. I asked him how long had Samantha been employed with the company and he confirmed "20 years". I asked him if Samantha had any prior violations to which he replied "No". We talked further, with basically me listening to him while he yelled and complained. I was finally able to get Danny to calm down a little and then I pled with him to not make a hasty decision. I asked him to please sleep on it and not fire her right then. He was hesitant, I could tell he did not like my recommendation; and that he wanted to go against my recommendation, but he finally agreed to sleep on the issue. "But I am still going to fire her tomorrow!" he said.

The advice I gave Danny could have saved him from making a bad decision.

The Mistake: Hastily firing employees while angry can lead to multiple issues, including:

• Not having enough time to research the issue.
• Failure to review the employee handbook, policies, and/or union contract.

- No documentation of the issues.
- Failure to secure a witness and/or security.
- Not taking time to consult with HR Representatives and/or Legal Counsel.

How to Fix the Mistake: Where possible, never terminate anyone while you are angry; unless it is a for safety or other issue that could negatively affect the workplace and/or the employees. Take the time to handle the termination, which should include the below five (5) steps:

1. Put the employee on notice that his or her behavior or conduct may lead to discipline;
2. Investigate;
3. Document;
4. Review gathered information with HR Representative and/or Legal Counsel; and
5. Prepare to terminate, if appropriate.

Please note: I am by no means advising you not to terminate an employee, or to wait for 30 days or so to terminate them; just give yourself some time to research and prepare. It can save you from expensive litigation.

Mistake

045 | INAPPROPRIATELY WITHHOLDING
MONEY
FROM AN EMPLOYEE'S
F I N A L   P A Y C H E C K

I hear it all the time, "Bonnie didn't turn in her uniform, could we withhold the uniform amount from her paycheck?" Or "Ralph didn't turn in his keys, we want to take it out of his last paycheck." Or "Carmen, left owing for the computer she used and won't return it. Should we take it out of her final paycheck."

These are very common questions. The answers are: "It depends on the state you live in and the circumstances."

The Mistake: Usually the employer is upset when the employee owes the company money and feels it is only right and fair to take it out of the employee's final paycheck. However, it is important to remember that unfortunately, right and fair in our eyes may not always be the legal way to conduct workplace business.

How to Fix the Mistake: Employers should be aware of their state law regarding taking deductions from an employee's paycheck. For example, I will use Michigan law, since I live in Michigan. According to the **State of Michigan website:** "Employers can make deductions required by law, i.e. taxes, Friend of the Court payments, and union dues. All other deductions require the employer to get employees' signed authorization before the deduction is made. The employer is required to itemize deductions on the pay stub."

To be more specific:

Deductions from Wages (Michigan Law)

An employee must consent in writing each time an employer makes a deduction from his or her wages, if the deduction is for the benefit of the employer. These type of deductions include:

• Cash shortages
• Breakage, damage, or loss of the employer's property
• Required uniforms
• Required tools
• Other items necessary for employment

Although an employer can deduct the above-listed items with the written consent of an employee, the employer cannot coerce or threaten the employee with discharge to obtain the written consent.

An employer cannot withhold or deduct wages from an employee's paycheck, unless:

• Required or permitted to do so by law,
• Required or permitted by a collective bargaining agreement, or
• The employee has consented in writing, without coercion, to the deduction.

Therefore, it is crucial to know your state law and to comply accordingly.

046 | NOT HOLDING MANAGEMENT **ACCOUNTABLE** **AND/OR COVERING UP** FOR BAD MANAGERS

I've worked with a few organizations where I observed management colluding together and even covering up for each other, on almost every issue. I recall one case in particular that involved the Director of Operations, Lisa. Lisa was a very ineffective Director. Unfortunately, she did not have the education nor experience required to perform her job duties/responsibilities; however she was hired because she was a good friend of the CEO. Lisa would just let things go. She would say, "I will take care of the issue later." But she rarely kept her word. Her subordinates would ask questions or request assistance; and in most cases, Lisa would say "Okay, I will be with you soon", but she almost never helped them. To make matters even worse, Lisa's attitude was bad and she was always on the defensive, probably because she knew she was not qualified for the job. Lisa's behavior caused stress to many of her employees and the departments that had to work with her. Needless to say, her department was in constant chaos.

I discussed the issue regarding Lisa with the CEO. He told me that Lisa was his friend and had grown up with him, all the way back to Junior High School. He promised to address the concerns about Lisa, but also stated he was going to stick by her. Unfortunately, he continued to ignore the constant complaints and hoped that the employees would just try harder to work with Lisa.

The Mistake: Unfortunately, sometimes management teams cover up for each other regarding many things, including sexual harassment, bullying, drugs/alcohol, pornography, etc., and it appears that some of them think it is the correct way to conduct business, the "Us against Them" mentality. Or, they may believe that it gives the appearance of management unity. Management unison could be great, if policies and procedures are followed appropriately. Typically, not holding management accountable or covering up for bad managers ends badly and can be costly to the overall organization.

How to Fix the Mistake: When discrimination is attributed to a supervisor with immediate or successively higher authority over employees, and the supervisor violates the law regarding an employee; i.e. commits a tangible adverse employment action or causes a hostile work environment; the employer may be delegated liable. Therefore, it is best for employers to focus on creating work environments where there are no tangible adverse employment actions; which can include implementing effective harassment policies and communicating those polices to employees frequently. It is also important to maintain an environment where everyone is held accountable for his or her actions as appropriate. In other words, it pays to lead by example and deal with issues properly.

047

FAILURE TO RETAIN AND/OR
DESTROY
RECORDS ACCORDING
T O   T H E   L A W

Generally an employer could establish the following retention periods for both electronic and paper-based records (be sure to review with HR or legal before implementing):

- Personnel – 7 years after termination.
- Medical/benefits – 6 years after plan year (except employee exposure records must be kept at least 30 years).
- I-9 Forms – 3 years after termination.
- Hiring records – 2 years after hiring decision.

Note: CBA's may limit amount of time to hold disciplines, notice of work violation, etc. Below is an At-A-Glance Record Retention Guideline form. Please note the applicable law in the 3rd column.

AT-A-GLANCE FEDERAL RECORD RETENTION GUIDELINES

Record	Retention Period	Applicable Law	Suggested Form/Folder
Hiring, promotion, demotion, transfer, selection of training, layoff recall, discipline, or discharge of any employee	1 year after action taken (2 years for federal contractors)	29CFR 1627.3 (b)(1)(ii)	Job Application, Performance Review, Payroll Status Change, Separation Notice, Exit Interview. Separation Agreement
Job Postings and Job Advertising, Job requests submitted to employment agencies	1 year	29CFR 1627.3 (b)(1)(vi)	Store in Job-file folder
Job Applications	1 Year (includes seasonal and temp workers)	29CFR 1627.3 (b)(1)(i)	Application of Employment
Job Descriptions	1 Year past the last action taken on document	29CFR 1627.3 -ADEA	Job Description folder
Solicited Resumes	1 year	29CFR 1627.3 (b)(1)(i)	Store in Job-file folder
Unsolicited Resumes	Not required to be kept, but recommended as good business practice	29CFR 1627.3 (b)(1)(i)	Store in Job-file folder
Screening Tests	1 year	29CFR 1627.3 (b)(1)(iv)	HR Assessment/ Employment Test

Drug Test Results – general industry Drug Tests -Transportaion Industry	1 year after action taken 5 years after action taken	29CFR 1627.3 (b)(1)(v) 49CFR 382.401	Confidential Employee Medical Records folder
Result of Physical Exam	1 year	29CFR 1627.3 (b)(2)(v)	Confidential Employee Medical Record folder
Payroll Reoords	5 Years from the last date of entry	29CFR 516.5 (a) -FLSA	Payroll Records Folder. W- 4, W-2, 1099
Basic employment and earnings records. including time sheets and wage rate tables	5 Years	29CFR 516.6 (a) -FLSA	Payroll Records folder
Employee Records, including name, address, date of birth, occupation, rate of pay, compensaion per week	4 years	29CFR 1627.3(a)	Document on and store in confidential employee record folder
Record of charges of discrimination and any personnel records relevant or pending charge	Until final disposition	29CFR 1627.3(b)(3)	Confidential employee records folder
Termination Records	< 150 employees, 1 year from termination date, >150 employees 2 years from termination date	29CFR 1602.14	Employee File, Termination Folder

048 | N O T
CONSIDERING ADA
ACCOMMODATIONS

Robin works for a company with less than 30 employees. Robin had been with the company for approximately 10 years, and unfortunately, had a heart attack while performing her job duties. About 2 months later, after she was treated for her condition, her Doctor released her and allowed her to "return to work"; however with restrictions. The employer said, "We don't have to honor the restrictions because we only have 30 employees and we don't have to comply with the Family and Medical Leave Act requirements." I agreed that the employer did not have to comply with FMLA, but I recommended that they have to consider the Americans with Disabilities Act (ADA).

The Mistake: Rushing to deny restrictions or terminating someone with restrictions can come back to haunt you. **Per the Equal Employment Opportunity Commission (EEOC),** "the ADA prohibits discrimination on the basis of disability in employment and requires that covered employers (employers with 15 or more employees) provide reasonable accommodations to applicants and employees with disabilities that require such accommodations due to their disabilities." Denying employees this right can lead to costly litigation and/or compliance fees and penalties.

How to Fix the Mistake: It is a good idea for employers to show good faith, if appropriate, and if it is not an undue hardship, to try to accommodate employees with a disability. Per the **EEOC Publication, Employer-Provided Leave and the Americans with Disabilities Act**, A reasonable accommodation is, generally, "any change in the work environment or in the way things are customarily done that enables an individual with a disability to enjoy equal employment opportunities." That can include making modifications to existing leave policies and providing leave when needed for a disability, even where an employer does not offer leave to other employees. As with any other accommodation, the goal of providing leave as an accommodation is to afford employees with disabilities equal employment opportunities."

Mistake

049 | INCONSISTENT DISCIPLINES AND **TURNING A BLINDS EYE TO CERTAIN EMPLOYEES'** VIOLATIONS

While reviewing disciplinary actions as part of an HR audit of a large health care organization; I noticed there were three (3) disciplinary actions administered for the same offense, but each employee had been issued a different level of discipline. The violation was sleeping on the job. One of the employees, a male, received a verbal warning, another employee, another male, was suspended for 3 days, and the other one, a female, was terminated. Because of the inconsistencies, I decided to look into it further.

After discussing the issue with the Director of Human Resources, I was told that the organization's practice was to allow management to use their own individual discretion in administering the level of discipline that they felt was best. The Director further indicated that a few employees did not receive any discipline at all for sleeping. I said, "Wow, I'm surprised you haven't been hit on this." The Director said, "Well if the managers like you and you do a good job, you probably won't get disciplined."

Really?

The Mistake : Allowing managers to make independent decisions regarding levels of disciplinary action; without considering the overall organization, is a mistake. We all have people we like and others we don't like as much; but in the workplace, that should not be a consideration when administering discipline. Also, I would not recommend ignoring disciplining an employee because they were a good worker. When a terminated employee ascertains that a co-worker received a lesser penalty for the same offence, you can expect litigation of some sort.

How to Fix the Mistake: Employers should be as consistent as possible when applying discipline. The organization should have a progressive disciplinary process and Human Resources should have a tracking mechanism of offenses and penalties. If for some reason, you cannot discipline consistently, it is essential to have detailed documentation explaining the reason for the inconsistency; to protect the organization.

050 | NOT PAYING ATTENTION TO TURNOVER

"We have a huge problem with turnover," said Jamarius, Director of Employment. "The overtime is through the roof, because we hire people and they quit," he said. "I don't know why they keep quitting." "How long has this been going on?" I asked. "For years, and it seems to be getting worse," he answered. "Do you have any idea why they quit?" I asked. Jamarius answered angrily, "They don't like to work that's why!"

While conducting the HR audit, I reviewed everything and spoke with many employees. The morale was low and the overtime was unbelievable. Several employees barely spent time at home with family. I quickly noted many easy fixes to the problem. It appeared that the turnover problem had simply been ignored.

The Mistake: Ignoring turnover causes morale issues. Employees may get more and more depressed about their job every time someone quits. They may even feel like they are victims for having to work at a company where everyone is quitting. They may also believe that the people who are able to quit are fortunate. Oftentimes, the employees look forward to the day they can leave the company as well and they sometimes get fixated on leaving.

Consider this...How productive will your team be under these circumstances? How excited are they going to be to serve customers? Probably not that much. When looking at the whole picture, turnover costs can be massive.

How to Fix the Mistake: Typically, the first thing I do is conduct an HR Audit. A well-managed HR Audit can quickly uncover issues. Please note, the employer can conduct exit interviews and surveys to help uncover the reasons why turnover exists. It is always a good idea to take a good look at the organization. Is it clean, does it have a good reputation? Taking the time to get a tune-up (HR Audit) is always a good idea. It is best not to ignore turnover, as ignoring it almost never turns out positive for the organization.

Mistake

051 | FAILURE TO CONDUCT INVESTIGATIONS BEFORE MAKING DECISIONS

I will never forget the day that Amalia complained that she was being sexually harassed by a coworker. I remember it so vividly because Amalia was about 70 years old and her complaint was against her 22-year old co-worker, Fernandez. My first thought was, no way. I asked her to explain what happened. And here's her story...

She would go to the break area and Fernandez would rub up against her and whisper in her ear. He would also hug her and touch her in a manner that was uncomfortable. Amalia said that she told Fernandez to stop bothering her, but he continued to harass her. She further stated that she did not know how Fernandez got her phone number, but he called her multiple times at home, asking her to "hook up." While listening to her, and of course keeping a poker face, I was in disbelief of her comments and really thought she might be delusional. However, even though, in my mind, I did not believe it happened; I immediately began conducting an investigation.

Guess what?! Her allegations were substantiated!

The Mistake: The mistake happens when employers ignore complaints based on opinions or subjective thoughts. When ALL complaints are not evaluated equally, it puts the organization at risk of expensive litigation.

How to Fix the Mistake: Employers should investigate complaints, including formal, informal, third party, etc.; even if the allegation seems far-fetched, or if the complainant is a chronic complainer. According to the **EEOC Guidelines** regarding investigations: "An employer should set up a mechanism for a prompt, thorough, and impartial investigation into alleged harassment. As soon as management learns about alleged harassment, it should determine whether a detailed fact-finding investigation is necessary. For example, if the alleged harasser does not deny the accusation, there would be no need to interview witnesses, and the employer could immediately determine appropriate corrective action."

The EEOC further states: "It may be necessary to undertake intermediate measures before completing the investigation to ensure that further harassment does not occur. Examples of such measures are making scheduling changes so as to avoid contact between the parties; transferring the alleged harasser; or placing the alleged harasser on non-disciplinary leave with pay pending the conclusion of the investigation. The complainant should not be involuntarily transferred or otherwise burdened, since such measures could constitute unlawful retaliation."

It is critical to take complaints seriously and investigate as appropriate. As we know, in HR, unbelievable situations happen all the time. Thus, it's best to err on the side of investigating issues to protect the organization.

052 WRITING SUBJECTIVE **DISCIPLINES** **A N D   O T H E R** DOCUMENTATION

Disciplinary actions can tell a lot about an employee, however the actions can also express a lot about the writer of the disciplinary action. Below are some of the comments I've read in corrective action forms over the years.

- "You have been here for 4 years, you should know better..."
- "You never listen, that is why you continue to make the same mistake"
- "DO NOT, I repeat, DO NOT come in late again or the consequences will be worse..."
- "You always start trouble and I am growing very tired of you acting crazy"
- "The time has finally come to terminate your employment..."
- "This is the last time you will get away with being sneaky...."

The Mistake: The mistake typically happens when employers write how they feel and/or their opinions of what happened. It is best to stick to the facts of what occurred. Also, it is never acceptable to write disciplines in a manner that can be construed as the employer exhibiting bias, discrimination, favoritism, etc.

How to Fix the Mistake: It is a good idea for employers to think of corrective actions as evidence in a jury trial. In order to determine what happened and make a decision, the jury needs to analyze the facts. For example, please review the scenarios below, which describe the same issue:

Example 1
Joe, on Monday, you came to work acting very weird. You were drunk from the night before. You always come in like that on Mondays. You are suspended for 3 days.

Example 2
Joe, on Monday, January 15, you arrived at work wearing a wrinkled uniform and you were stumbling and almost fell on the bookshelf. Your eyes were blood red and you had an odor about you that appeared to be alcohol. The HR Manager and I called you in the office and asked you if you were under the influence. You said "No, absolutely not!" We asked you to take an alcohol level test, for your safety. You refused ....

...........Joe, your behavior on January 15 was insubordination. You are (suspended or terminated or...whatever you determine is best)

Which scenario do you think the Jury would better understand, as well as feel the employer's pain, regarding Joe's behavior? I hope you answered Example #2. Also, please note, in Example #1, if the jury discovers that Joe was on time for work on just one Monday, how would that change the statement? The jury just might discount the entire corrective action.

053 | NOT PROPERLY FOLLOWING FMLA REGULATIONS

I held a community training session for employers regarding Family and Medical Leave Act (FMLA) abuse. I went over all the steps of FMLA, had a group exercise, video, etc. After class, a few employers signed up for our services and Winston became a new client. Winston had a few cases of suspected FMLA abuse. He called me on several occasions and I explained how to handle the situations.

A month later Winston called me regarding the same employee we previously spoke about. We revisited the FMLA steps to make sure he was compliant. I asked Winston if he wanted to review the information from the training session and he replied, "No," and he shared that "while I was speaking with a colleague about all the steps, they basically told me that sending letters and correspondence was FMLA overkill and I don't really have to do all that, so I don't do all of that. I can just get rid of her." I was floored. So I said, respectfully, "Well, Winston, that "overkill" is the law."

The Mistake: Cutting corners is not the best practice when dealing with FMLA. If the FMLA law is not followed appropriately, it could be perceived as FMLA interference, a violation of the law. For example, in 2013, a well-know hospital, in Michigan, had to pay a former employee approximately $423,500 because the jury ruled that the hospital terminated the employee in violation of properly following FMLA regulations. In some instances, when damages are awarded in FMLA-related cases, Judges can rule to double the amount of damages.

How to Fix the Mistake: Employers should be verse and knowledgeable in FMLA law. HR Professionals should be thoroughly trained on the FMLA processes. Also, employers should keep good records or use software to track FMLA information. All correspondence should be sent to employees as appropriate. For help with the FMLA steps and processes, employers can access the **US Department of Labor's FMLA Advisor. The website, http://webapps.dol.gov/elaws/fmla.htm,** provides guidance and steps to determining eligibility and identifies employer responsibilities.

If FMLA administration is too time consuming for the organization or too confusing; consider outsourcing the FMLA administration duties to the experts.

Mistake

054 | NOT AUDITING YOUR HR DEPARTMENT

I was contacted by the COO, Lee, of an organization with over 200 employees. Lee complained that the company had excessive absenteeism, multiple employees out on FMLA, and low morale. Lee told me that a few of his key people, in hard to fill positions, left and another one might leave. He shared that his profits were suffering and he was not sure what to do next. I asked him several questions about the company. I then suggested we conduct an HR Audit.

The audit revealed multiple problems and issues with HR practices and policies. I also uncovered compliance issues. Basically several things were simmering...and about to BLOW-UP! I estimated that the organization saved hundreds of thousands of dollars or more by conducting the audit and by making our recommended adjustments/changes.

The Mistake: Oftentimes HR staff is so busy performing the day-to-day functions that many issues get neglected. Unfortunately, neglected issues can increase company risk levels. It only takes one disgruntled employee to file a complaint of unfair labor practices to incite a full blown investigation by the IRS, DOL, EEOC, etc. These investigations interrupt organizations, as well as are time-consuming and very expensive. Allowing high-risk issues and practices to continue can quickly lead to expensive litigation and/or compliance violations.

How to Fix the Problem: Conducting an HR Audit can help organizations avoid litigation and non-compliance fines. An HR Audit can also provide an objective look at the company's human resources policies, practices, procedures, programs, systems, and strategies to help protect the company from litigation and fines. An HR Audit can also facilitate and establish best practices, identify opportunities for improvement, and evaluate outsourcing options. HR Audits can ensure effective utilization of HR resources and improve customer service, which in turn can add to the bottom line.

Additionally, HR Audits assist with compliance, consistency, and appropriate processes. Certain HR functions can save a business a considerable amount of money. In other words, HR can add to your bottom line through cost-saving measures. Therefore it makes good business sense to assess your HR department policies, practices, procedures, systems, etc. to ensure HR is as effective and efficient as possible.

055 | FAILING TO CHECK EMPLOYEE ELIGIBILITY FOR FMLA

Regularly, I've been contacted by clients regarding FMLA issues. When I review the FMLA information, I am amazed at how many of the employees were not even eligible for FMLA. I would say probably 25% of them were not eligible. I remember one client in particular, Sharon. While conducting a comprehensive training on FMLA for Sharon and her staff, I placed emphasis on making sure employees were eligible. A few months later, Sharon contracted me with questions about an employee out on FMLA. Guess what I found? You guessed it; the employee was not eligible.

The Mistake: Typically the employer forgets to check the 12 months service requirement and/or if the employee has not worked 1,250 hours. When employers mistakenly allow employees to go on FMLA leave, because they are not eligible, it can cost the organization in administrative time, replacement costs, overtime costs, etc.
Please note: If the employer chooses to give an employee FMLA leave, who is not eligible per the law; the employer is allowed to do so, however the employer should be consistent with all employees.

How to Fix the Mistake: When FMLA is requested or possibly required, before issuing the certification paperwork, please check the employee's eligibility.

For a refresher, please review the following:

Eligibility
An employee of a covered employer is eligible for leave if the employee has been employed by the employer under all the following conditions:

- For at least 12 months.
- For at least 1,250 hours of service during the previous 12-month period.
- At a worksite where the employer employs at least 50 employees within 75 miles of the worksite.

Qualifying Events

The FMLA provides eligible employees protected, unpaid leave for the following qualifying events:

- Birth and care of the employee's newborn son or daughter (regardless of whether the employee is female or male).
- Placement of a son or daughter with the employee for adoption or foster care.
- Times when the employee is needed to care for a spouse, son, daughter or parent with a serious health condition.
- Times when an employee is unable to perform the functions of his or her job because of a serious health condition.
- Any qualifying exigency arising out of the fact that the employee's spouse, son, daughter or parent is a covered service member on active duty (or has been notified of an impending call or order to active duty).
- Caring for a covered service member with a serious injury or illness if the employee is the spouse, son, daughter, parent or next of kin of the service member.

Serious Health Condition

Under the FMLA, a "serious health condition" (SHC) is an illness, injury, impairment, or physical or mental condition that involves either of the following:

- Inpatient care in a hospital, hospice or residential medical care facility.
- Continuing treatment by a health care provider.

It is essential for employers to check FMLA eligibility to avoid unnecessary costs.

056 | NOT COORDINATING FMLA, ADA, AND WORKERS COMPENSATION

The Director of Operations of a large manufacturing company notified me that one of their production workers hurt his arm while working on the assembly line. The Director further stated the production worker might need surgery on his arm.

This is a situation where you may have to coordinate FMLA, ADA, and Workers Compensation.

The Mistake: It is recommended to run FMLA concurrent with a Workers' Compensation absence. If an employer fails to designate Workers Compensation absences as FMLA leave, the employer could potentially provide the employee with more leave than they would normally be entitled. Additionally, while the employee is on FMLA, the employer is required to continue to provide benefits at the same level prior to the employee's leave. Also, once an employee uses their 12 weeks of FMLA leave, the employees' Workers Compensation benefit status does not provide employees with job protection.

Therefore, when an employer does not coordinate FMLA, ADA, and Workers Compensation, the employer could suffer unnecessary costs.

How to Fix the Mistake: Employers should educate themselves and be knowledgeable to the three laws, FMLA, ADA, and Workers Compensation; and how the laws work together. Please see the table below:

FMLA	ADA	Workers Compensation
Sets minimum leave standards for employees regarding:	Prohibits discrimination against applications and employees who:	Provides for payment of compensation and rehabilitation for workplace injuries and minimize employer liability for:
• Birth of a child, to care for a newborn, or placement for adoption or foster care of a child; • "Serious health condition" that makes the employee unable to perform one or more of the essential functions of the employee's job; • To care for a spouse, child, or parent with a serious health condition	• Have a physical or mental impairment that substantially limits one or more major life activities; • Have a record of such an impairment; or • Are regarded as having such an impairment	• Personal injuries that arise out of and in the course of employment.

Therefore, it is a best practice for employers to always coordinate the three laws when appropriate.

Mistake

057 | IMPROPERLY HANDLING OF **PREGNANT** EMPLOYEES' CONDITIONS

Jamie, Office Manager, called me regarding an employee who was pregnant. She stated the employee had only worked for the company for three (3) months and she further stated that the employee "knew she was pregnant when we interviewed her and did not tell us until she started working. We were already short and cannot afford to have her here. Can we terminate her for false interview or how can we fire her?"

The Mistake: In 2015, the **Supreme Court ruled, in Young v. UPS,** that pregnant employees have the same right to accommodations as employees "similar in their ability or inability to work," using a traditional comparator analysis. Additionally, the Pregnancy Discrimination Act requires that employers treat pregnant women "the same for all employment-related purposes . . . as other persons not so affected but similar in their ability or inability to work." It is this clause that the Supreme Court's decision in Young v. UPS interpreted. **(http://www.scotusblog.com/case-files/cases/young-v-united-parcel-service/)**

Violating this law can cause discrimination litigation; which can be expensive as it can include: Attorney fees, investigative expenses, lost productivity, etc. Additionally, if it is determined that the employer habitually involved discriminatory practices; the judge may order the employer to pay all attorney fees for both parties. There can also be punitive damages, back pay, and restoration of the employee's job.

How to Fix the Mistake: Typically, if employers provide any accommodations, they should provide accommodation for pregnant workers as described in the Pregnancy Discrimination Act. (Please remember to always consider your state laws as well). Also, employers should monitor consistency in accommodations throughout the organization.

058 | FAILURE TO PROPERLY REVIEW FMLA
CERTIFICATION PAPERWORK

Veronica, one of my VIP clients, called and asked me if I could stop by her office because she had an FMLA issue. I said sure and scheduled a time to meet with her. Veronica told me that the employee in question had been off work for six (6) weeks on FMLA. She further told me she had received Facebook posts showing several pictures of the employee at a party. The employee appeared to be having a great time on the pictures and Veronica was livid. I asked Veronica to allow me to review the employee's FMLA certification and other pertinent information in order to advise her on the next steps.

As I reviewed the paperwork, I noticed, on the certification paperwork, by the line that reads: Relationship of family member to you, the employee had written "Aunt." I read it again and it said "Aunt." After further review, it was determined that the employee was not eligible.

The Mistake: Oftentimes employers receive the FMLA certification information but never really review the paperwork. In the scenario above, the employee received six (6) weeks of leave without being eligible for FMLA. Therefore the employer most likely incurred unnecessary expenses by having to cover the employee's job, and probably had to pay overtime.

How to Fix the Mistake: Employers should always take a magnifying glass to the certification paperwork and should be knowledgeable to the FMLA law. To refresh, covered Employers must grant 12 workweeks, unpaid leave to eligible employees for:

• The birth and care of a newborn child of the employee;
• The placement with the employee of a son or daughter for adoption or foster care;

- Caring for a spouse, son, daughter, or parent with a serious health condition;
- Taking medical leave when the employee is unable to work because of a serious health condition; or
- For qualifying exigencies arising regarding employee's son, daughter, or parent is on active duty or call to
- Active duty status

There are a few exceptions, such as in loco parentis; which typically refers to a person who assumes parental status and carries out the obligations of a parent to a child with whom he or she may have no legal or biological connection. But, in loco parentis also applies to an employee who wants to take time off to care for an individual who stood in loco parentis for the employee when he or she was a child. It also applies to leave for qualifying exigencies as stated in FMLA regulation 825.215 (a)(5) and to military caregiver leave per Regulation 825.127 (1) and (2). Although Section 825.122(c)(3) of FMLA regulations states that in loco parentis status requires the employee to provide both financial support or care for a child.

Therefore, in the scenario above, an employee probably could take leave to care for his or her Aunt with a serious health condition, if the Aunt was responsible for the employee's day-to-day care when the employee was a child.

125

Mistake

059 | NOT HAVING A CLEAR UNDERSTANDING **OF WHEN EMPLOYEES ARE ON OR OFF THE CLOCK,** AND KNOWING WHAT IS COMPENSABLE

In 2013, Entertainer Lady Gaga was sued, by her former personal assistant (salaried) to recover almost $380,000 in overtime for on-call time (in addition to her annual salary of $75,000), O'Neill v Meermaid Touring, Inc. According to both parties, O'Neill was expected to be available as needed throughout each hour of each day. Some of the many tasks the singer expected of the personal assistant included:

- Serving as Lady Gaga's "personal alarm clock".
- Ensuring that Lady Gaga kept to her schedule.
- Making sure costumes were available for performances.
- Having towels ready after showers.
- Ensuring "special food" was available for her on demand at every location.
- Making sure Lady Gaga had ample time for hairstyling, make-up and voice warm-ups.
- Monitoring email and telephone communications.
- Handling luggage (usually about 20 bags).
- Assisting with costume changes, arranging for ice packs, and on and on...

Lady Gaga moved to dismiss the case but the Judge refused, because he felt there was enough factual dispute regarding whether the on-call time was "work" (meaning was Ms. O'Neill was so restricted during that time that she could not attend to her own affairs).

After the Judge's statement, the parties settled for an undisclosed amount of cash. (Huffington Post)

The Mistake: Under the Fair Labor Standards Act (FLSA), employees are entitled to be paid for time spent actually working.

This includes work at home, travel for work, waiting time, training, and probationary periods; and work beyond a normal workweek schedule, even if the employee volunteered to stay and/or did not obtain advance approval to stay. To avoid the obligations of the Act, a person must be completely relieved of duty.

Another mistake employers make is in distinguishing between Wait Time and On-Call time. The question here is whether the employee has been engaged to wait (compensable) or is waiting to be engaged (not compensable). An employee is "engaged to wait" and on duty when "waiting is an integral part of the job" 29 CFR 785.15. On the other hand, an employee is "waiting to be engaged," and not on compensable time when he or she is "completely relieved of duty" and where that period is "long enough to enable him to use the time effectively for his or her own purposes. 29 CFR 785.16(a)

Not understanding the distinctions could land employers in very hot water. And if the same mistake is made habitually, it can be a huge cost to the employer.

How To Fix the Mistake: The mistake can be fixed with management training and/or a point person to make FLSA determinations. There is a two-part test that courts use to determine if wait time is compensable time, which is:

1. Is the wait time predominantly for the employer's benefit?
2. Can the employee effectively use the waiting time for their own benefit?

Similarly, for on-call time:

1. On call time is compensable if the employee is required to remain on-call on the employer's premises.
2. Alternatively, the "on-call" time is not compensable if the employee is permitted to either remain on-call at home, or provide a message number where he ``r she can be reached.

The general premise is whether or not the employer controls the on-call time or whether the employee is free to use the time for personal pursuits.

Mistake

060 | LACK OF UNDERSTANDING THE **DIFFERENCE BETWEEN "JUST OBNOXIOUS BEHAVIOR"** AND "ILLEGAL CONDUCT"

Tim White loved to flirt with the ladies in the office. That was just his style. He would wink at the women, tell them they looked nice, and tap them on their shoulders while nodding his approval. He talked loud to impress the women and he even told jokes that were almost inappropriate. He enjoyed speaking to women at close range.

Is this behavior "just obnoxious" or "illegal conduct"?

The Mistake: Sometimes it can be difficult to differentiate between "just obnoxious behavior" and "illegal conduct". Because it is difficult, many employers write it off as "That's just Tim being Tim." Therefore, the employer simply ignores the behavior; which could cost the employer in the future.

How to Fix the Mistake: The factors that differentiate between "just obnoxious behavior" and "illegal conduct" are:

- Whether the conduct results in a tangible employment action; and
- Whether the conduct is unwelcome and can be considered objectively hostile.

As for (1), it is a good idea for employers to keep an eye out for seemingly unusual employee behaviors and actions. Inappropriate actions should be heavily documented.

As for (2), it is recommended that employers seriously consider and investigate any complaint, report, or mention of conduct or behavior of which an employee feels uncomfortable.

The EEOC states:

"Prevention is the best tool to eliminate harassment in the workplace. Employers are encouraged to take appropriate steps to prevent and correct unlawful harassment. They should clearly communicate to employees that unwelcome harassing conduct will not be tolerated. They can do this by establishing an effective complaint or grievance process, providing anti-harassment training to their managers and employees, and taking immediate and appropriate action when an employee complains. Employers should strive to create an environment in which employees feel free to raise concerns and are confident that those concerns will be addressed. Employers are encouraged to inform the harasser directly that the conduct is unwelcome and must stop. Employees should also report harassment to management at an early stage to prevent its escalation. https://www.eeoc.gov/laws/types/harassment.cfm

Because there is such a thin line between "just obnoxious behavior" and "illegal conduct," employers should prevent questionable conduct, behaviors, and actions to avoid liability.

061 | FAILURE TO REINSTATE EMPLOYEES ON FMLA LEAVE TO THE SAME OR SIMILAR POSITION

When conducting FMLA training classes, I typically test employers using the below scenario:

Peggy Smith is a Production Manager at ABC Manufacturing Company. Peggy notifies ABC that she is going on maternity leave. She completes her certification paperwork appropriately and submits it 30 days in advance. Peggy then takes 12-weeks FMLA leave.

During Peggy's absence, Jennifer Long performs Peggy's job and does an exceptional job; she's more efficient than Peggy. In fact, Jennifer successfully cut costs, reorganizes the department, and increases production; which in turn improves efficiency and increases revenue.

The VP of ABC notices Jennifer's stellar performance; however, is also aware that Peggy was a substandard performer who did just enough to get by. The VP feels it is in the best interest of the company to retain Jennifer in the position. As a result of this decision, the VP determines that when Peggy returns, she will be placed in a position that is lower than her previous position; however, Peggy will be paid at the same rate. Can the VP do this?

The Mistake: The above scenario happens frequently. When an employee goes on leave, oftentimes the employer wants to replace them for various reasons. "Employers may reinstate the employee to his or her former position or to an equivalent position. In practice, however, this doesn't give employers much leeway: The equivalent position must be virtually identical, in every important respect, to the employee's former position." (Guerin, Lisa; England, Deborah C. (2015-07-21). Essential Guide to Family & Medical Leave, The (p.

247). NOLO. Kindle Edition.) Therefore, in the above scenario, Peggy's new position should have the same prestige as her former position.

How to Fix the Mistake: It is recommended that employers understand and follow the FMLA law. If possible, a designated Human Resources representative(s) or assigned staff member(s) should handle all of the FMLA claims to ensure consistency in application.

Additionally, it is also suggested that employers have access to a human resources expert and/or legal counsel to assist in interpreting the FMLA law, as well as help with decision making.

062 | NOT CONSIDERING OUTSOURCING HR SERVICES

"Marjorie, our HR Manager, suddenly quit. She performed all of the organizations' Family and Medical Leave Act (FMLA) tracking and paperwork duties. Renee, the HR Coordinator is very knowledgeable; however, she had never worked with FMLA. This is a big problem because I don't know how quickly we can hire someone to replace Marjorie," said Phil, the Director of Operations.

My comment to Phil, "You can outsource the FMLA tasks and take your time replacing Marjorie. I'm pretty sure you will save money and on top of that get expert assistance. As a matter of fact, lets take a look at your employee roster and workflow. There may be other outsource opportunities available. You might not even need to replace Marjorie, which could be an additional savings for you." Phil was amazed, he never really considered outsourcing. After he completed the process, he was very happy indeed.

The Mistake: Many employers ignore or just can't get their arms around the ability to save money by outsourcing time consuming tasks. Additionally, many business strategies suffer unnecessarily by employers stretching their staff too thin and/or requiring them to perform tasks, in which they are not qualified. Outsourcing those tasks can not only save time and money, they can give employers access to expertise in the field, as well as to technological advancements.

How to Fix the Mistake: Employers should at least consider outsourcing opportunities when making decision. It's a good idea to evaluate the pros and cons, i.e., cost savings, company expertise, time-savings, etc.

The Society for Human Resources Management (SHRM), the world's largest HR professional society, conducted a survey of hundreds of companies regarding their outsourcing habits. The charts below illustrate what SHRM found to be typical HR Outsourced Functions and the most common reasons that companies outsource. (www.shrm.org)

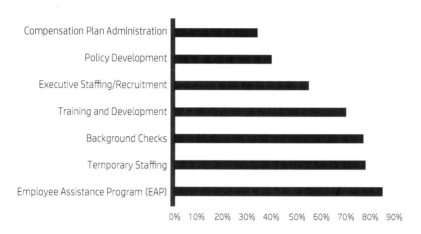

TYPICAL HR FUNCTIONS OUTSOURCED

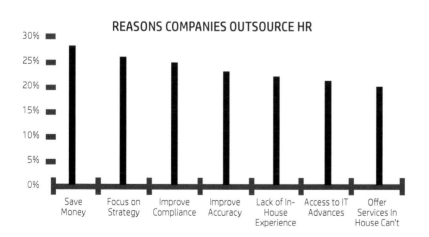

REASONS COMPANIES OUTSOURCE HR

Therefore, to be as efficient as possible, outsourcing is considered a viable and cost saving option.

Mistake

FAILURE TO ACCOMMODATE
EMPLOYEES'
TEMPORARY DISABILITIES

Phyllis submitted Family and Medical Leave Act Certification paperwork indicating she was having knee replacement surgery. On the certification paperwork, Phyllis's physician noted that she would need 12-weeks for recuperation. In the 10-week of her recuperation, Phyllis's employer sent her a letter indicating the expiration date of the FMLA and inquiring about her return to work prior to week 12.

Still recovering after 12-weeks, Phyllis's physician extended her leave for an additional 4-weeks. Phyllis followed the company policy regarding calling off work. 3-weeks into the extension, Phyllis received a letter from her employer indicating that she had been terminated based on the attendance policy. The termination papers specifically stated she had missed more than 8-days in one year; therefore in violation of the attendance policy resulting in termination of her employment.

Is the employer correct?

The Mistake: The mistake was not considering if Phyllis needed an accommodation, per the Americans With Disabilities Act (ADA). Phyllis was temporarily disabled and may have needed an accommodation; however, the employer quickly terminated her as soon as she was in violation of the attendance policy. The employer's practice, in this case, could quickly land the employer in court.

How to Fix the Mistake: The employer should consider the ADA law, and should enter into the interactive process to determine if an accommodation is required. A key step to determining if an accommodation is necessary transpires during the interactive process; which involves the employee and the employer. This process is described in the EEOC regulation found at 29 CFR 1630.9. Employers can also determine if the accommodation is proper or if it is an undue hardship by performing the following steps:

SUCCESSFUL ACCOMODATION

Step 1: Recognizing an Accomodation Request

Step 2: Gathering Information

Step 3: Exploring Accommodation Options

Step 4: Choosing an Accommodation

Step 5: Implementing the Accommodation

Step 6: Monitoring the Accommodation

It is recommended that the process be well-documented and that chosen accommodations be monitored. There may also need to be an expiration date for the accommodation to reevaluate:

- The employees' continued need for accommodation(s), or
- To determine if the accommodation(s) is no longer needed and can be removed, or
- If an alternate accommodation is needed, or
- To communicate if the accommodation caused a hardship.

064 | MAKING IMPROPER DEDUCTIONS
FROM EXEMPT EMPLOYEES' PAY

XYZ Manufacturing Company prematurely depleted their inventory supply. Because the company did not have inventory to perform work, the company shut down and the staff was sent home, without pay, for 2 days. The Director of Facilities, Jeanette, (exempt employee) was also not paid.

Jeannette was extremely upset about her pay reduction and complained to the CEO. "I did not get my full pay and this really hurts my finances. At this rate, I won't be able to pay my daughter's tuition for the semester." The CEO replied, "I am not going to pay you for not working 2 days. The building is closed. There is no work!"

Is the CEO correct?

The Mistake: The mistake is not fully understanding the Fair Labor Standards Act (FLSA) law and the criteria for exempt employees. Exempt Employees are employees who meet one of the FLSA exemption tests and who are paid on a fixed salary basis, and are not entitled to overtime. Per **U.S. Department of Labor Fact Sheet #17G**, to be paid on a salary basis means the employee "regularly receives a predetermined amount constituting all or part of the employee's salary, which amount is not subject to reduction because of variations in the quality or quantity of work performed."

Deductions from the salary of an exempt employee are generally prohibited. Except as set forth below, an exempt employee must receive the full salary for any week in which the employee performs any work, without regard to the number of days or hours worked. The exceptions provided by federal law are below:

Prohibited Deductions are:

- Partial day absences (except FMLA leave).
- Deductions for variations in the quantity or quality of work.
- Deductions for absences created or caused by the employer or by the operating requirements of the business (for example, when the employee is ready, willing and able to work, but work is not available).

Penalties

Employers that do not comply with FLSA's exemption provisions are subject to penalties, including:

- Payment of back wages
- Fines of up to $1,925 per violation in the case of willful or repeated violations of minimum wage and overtime provisions
- Injunctions preventing the sale, delivery, transportation, or shipment of goods produced by employees in violation of the law
- Criminal convictions: Employers may be **fined up to $11,000 for a first conviction and up to $11,000 and/or imprisoned up to six (6) months** for a second conviction.

How to Fix the Mistake: Employers, including finance and payroll personnel should be proficient in the proper methods to deduct pay from exempt employees. Employers generally cannot change exempt employees' compensation because of absences from work. However, employers can reduce pay without jeopardizing employees' exempt status if the following occur:

Proper Deductions may be made for:

- One or more full day absences for personal reasons, other than sickness and disability.
- One or more full day absences because of sickness or disability if such deductions are made under a bona fide plan, practice or policy of providing wage replacement benefits for these types of absences.
- Unpaid leave taken pursuant to the Family and Medical Leave Act (FMLA), including intermittent or partial day leave.
- To offset payment amounts for jury duty, witness fees and military pay (but not for travel and parking).
- Penalties or suspensions made in good faith for violations of written safety rules of "major significance."
- Full day disciplinary suspensions imposed in good faith for violations of written work place conduct rules, but not for performance or attendance problems.

- Whatever day(s) of the first and last weeks of employment the employee does not work.

Additionally, there is no requirement that the predetermined salary of an exempt employee be paid if the employee performs no work at all for the entire workweek.

Mistake

065 | REHIRING EMPLOYEES WHO WERE FIRED

Demarko, owner of an upscale hospitality company, was experiencing a sudden and substantial decline in revenue. He couldn't understand why he was losing so much money. He noted that the patron attendance was about the same as the year before and his employee count was similar to the prior year. As he continued to search for a reasonable explanation to the revenue decline, he soon discovered that his manager was ordering almost twice the amount of supplies compared to the previous year.

Demarko questioned his manager regarding the increased orders, and the manager's response was, "I only order what is needed to operate. No more, no less" At that point, Demarko believed that someone was stealing from him; therefore, decided to install surveillance equipment. He also decided to monitor the back door of his company from a room in a hotel across the street. At that point, I began to refer to him as "Columbo"; you know, from the detective show "Columbo".

Demarko began his stakeout in the early hours of the morning. He watched and watched. He saw his manager arrive early, as he always did, to start setting up for the day. He then observed the unbelievable! His manager exited the rear of the building pushing a large cart of merchandise out to his car and loading it up with company supplies. Demarko was shocked! Needless to say, the manager was fired.

Approximately two months later, I visited Demarko. During my visit, I noticed the manager who had been fired; still working. Puzzled, I asked Demarko if he had rehired the manager. His reply, "Yes. He was the only one who could do the job."

Well, about 8 months later, that same manager sued Demarko for half a million dollars. He didn't win that much, but he won quite a bit.

The Mistake:
The mistake is not believing that anyone can be replaced. If you don't agree with that, think about what you would do if a key employee passed away. You would most likely hire someone else, or find alternative methods to get things done, or outsource, etc.

Oftentimes terminated employees become angry and resentful, even if their termination was deserved. If you bring them back, they may have revenge on their minds and spend most of their time trying to take down the employer. This is an extremely costly mistake.

How to Fix the Mistake:
Please don't rehire people who have been involuntary terminated, unless the termination was for a very minor issue (and I still don't think it's a good idea). If you absolutely need to hire them back, I recommend involving HR and/or legal counsel for advice.

Mistake

066 | UTILIZING GENERIC PERFORMANCE EVALUATIONS

When evaluating organizations, I often see forms similar to the performance review evaluation form below, for ALL staff members:

Performance Evaluation

Performance Factors	5	4	3	2	1
Job Knowledge					
Work Quality					
Work Quantity					
Teamwork					
Attendance/Dependability					
Appearance					

Does the above form adequately depict employee performance? Is it detailed enough to help employees improve?

The Mistake: Not aligning the performance review to the job descriptions and company mission is a mistake. Employees need to have a clear picture of company expectations as well as how they are performing. Providing more detailed information can increase productivity and profits. Additionally, it is a good idea to have a different performance evaluation form for management; who should be evaluated based on accomplishments and performance measures/metrics.

How to Fix the Mistake: Performance evaluations should align with the job descriptions and clearly define expectations to ensure employees perform as required and to meet company goals/mission. For example, below is an excerpt from a job description for Product Packer in a packing company.

Job Quality
Examines and inspects products and boxes in order to ensure that packing specifications are met. Maintains accurate records and cross checks product packing to ensure the right products are packed. Produces a significant volume of work efficiently in a specified period of time. Ability to work independently, with little or no direction/follow-up; timely completes tasks/ job assignments.

In the above example, the employee will know exactly what is expected of him or her and how he or she will be rated. Additionally, employers should use the performance review opportunity to not only rate employees but to provide coaching and constructive criticism; as well as include employees' accomplishments and plainly describe how the employee can be more valuable to the organization.

It is also recommended that the performance review be created to ensure a performance driven organization instead of being seniority based (if possible). For example, wage increases will be administered for employee performance instead of the employee's years of service.

If done correctly, profits could soar!

NOT CONDUCTING
E X I T
INTERVIEWS

"We have a morale problem and a turnover issue," said Max, the HR Director of an educational organization. "May I review your exit interviews?" I asked. "We don't do exit interviews." Max replied.

The Mistake: An employee resigning or retiring from your organization often has a lot of knowledge about the workplace. A final-sit down with a separating employee could prove valuable to your organization moving forward and may provide an outlet by allowing the leaving employee to "let off steam," which may possibly reduce the likelihood of a lawsuit.

An exit interview is the one of the best opportunities an organization can institute to receive honest, unbiased feedback, as well as encouraging the separating employee to disclose information that may protect the organization. Information collected can be of vital importance and can be used to assist in analyzing employee retention and turnover. It is a mistake and lost opportunity to not conduct exit interviews.

How to Fix the Mistake: It can really help the organization's performance by conducting exit interviews. Remember, the departing employee has nothing to lose by telling the truth about management practices, company culture, etc. The leaving employee may also shed light on unlawful and unethical issues within the workplace, such as sexual harassment, discrimination, bullying, etc.

Therefore, it is highly recommended to conduct exit interviews. It is also important to really listen to the leaving employee, document accordingly, and take action as needed.

FAILURE OF MANAGEMENT

068 | TO LEAD

BY EXAMPLE

Luis was the Director of Operations at a major medical center. It was common knowledge that Luis did not really like his job and he had a very negative attitude. The employees knew that they would pretty much be able to do what ever they wanted to do on Monday and Friday because Luis would almost always call off of work on those dates.

Luis' Director, who also missed a lot of work, decided to assign all of the Family and Medical Leave Act (FMLA) administration compliance duties to Luis. After learning the intricate details of FMLA, Luis decided to go to his doctor, pretend he had an illness, and get certified for FMLA coverage. Once Luis was approved for FMLA, he began taking intermittent FMLA time off from work on Monday, Tuesday, and Friday of many weeks.

The employees noticed Luis' pattern. Some of the employees commented that "if Luis doesn't care, neither do I" and "Why bother working when the boss doesn't work," and on and on. Thereby, when Luis was off, employees did not perform their job assignments as required, which led to a huge decrease in productivity.

Get the picture?

The Mistake: When management fails to lead appropriately, employees tend to follow their lead. If management doesn't follow rules, most employees won't follow rules. If management lies and cheats, many employees will lie and cheat. If management violates the law, so may employees. Not leading by example is a huge mistake, which can prove costly over time for employers.

How to Fix the Mistake: It is vital that employers project a positive image to employees. In order to lead by example, Employers should not:

- Use profanity,
- Habitually lie to staff,
- Be late all the time,
- Become intoxicated at company events,
- Be careless with equipment,
- Break the rules and/or the law,
- Bully or harass others,
- And other bad things, Etc.

It is a proven fact, that when management displays ethical, fair practices and follows the rules and the law, productivity peaks.

Mistake

069 | OVERLOOKING EMPLOYEES WHO ARE UNDER THE INFLUENCE

While conducting an HR Audit for a large non-profit organization, an employee shared with me that Tanya, the Project Manager, was an alcoholic and stated Tanya sometimes drank alcohol in her office and had even been found sleeping in her office. The employee then shared pictures of Tanya under the influence. I asked the employee if he had informed management about this matter. The employee stated he had reported it to his Director and the CEO, but, he said, "they laughed about it and did not take action." I was surprised by his response and asked him if he had any idea why they laughed. The employee answered, "They laughed because they feel like it is not a big deal."

Please don't let this be you...

The Mistake: Allowing employees to work under the influence of alcohol and/or drugs places the organization at risk. An employee under the influence can get hurt or cause others to get hurt; which, in turn can cost the company when faced with litigation and/or government evaluation.

How to Fix the Mistake: It is highly recommended that employers have policies regarding employees who are under the influence on the job. The policy should include how employees can report others in the workplace that are under the influence. The policy should also include how to report issues and with whom to report the issues. Employees under the influence should be handled based on organizational policies, procedures, and processes.

Mistake

070 | ALLOWING EMPLOYEES TO CONSUME ALCOHOL **AT COMPANY** PARTIES/EVENTS

"Vanessa, we've exceeded our numbers for the year!" said Jeremy, CEO of an IT company. "Our employees did a tremendous job and we want to have a party to celebrate the employees," he said. "We also want to provide alcohol so they can really let their hair down and enjoy themselves."

Is this a good idea?

The Mistake: Organizations have parties that provide alcohol all the time. They have holiday parties, celebrate new accounts, give retirement parties, etc. The mistake happens when employers don't take the time to think about the liability and they fail to plan accordingly. Not addressing these things can lead to costly problems.

How to Fix the Mistake: On the one hand, office holiday parties can build morale, offer opportunities for more casual interactions among workers, and reward employees for a productive year–but, on the other hand, they can be a source of liability for the organization. If employers choose to celebrate with alcohol, please consider the following tips to help keep the employer, and the employees safe:

• Review the insurance coverage before the party.
• If the party will be hosted onsite, determine whether the organization is covered for injuries or damage to property if alcohol is served on the premises. Employers may need to

purchase separate special event coverage or an additional liquor liability policy.

- For gatherings held offsite, such as in a restaurant, employers should request a copy of the venue's certificate of insurance and determine if additional coverage is needed.
- Don't make attendance at the party mandatory. Employees should understand that no work will be conducted at the party.
- Make it clear, before the party, that overindulgence and other offensive behavior are not acceptable.
- Remind employees that alcohol is no excuse for illegal or inappropriate behavior, such as sexual harassment.
- Consult your employee handbook and make sure that any company-sponsored festivities are not in violation of the policies in your handbook (such as those relating to an alcohol-free workplace).

Also:

- Avoid open bars.
- Approve the types of drinks that will be served in advance and consider the effects. According to the Centers for Disease Control and Prevention, one 12-ounce beer has about the same amount of alcohol as one 5-ounce glass of wine, or a 1.5-ounce shot of liquor.
- Consider a cash bar or provide a limited number of "free drink" tickets to each employee.
- Be sure there are a variety of non-alcoholic drinks available as well.
- Stop offering alcohol at least 1 hour before the party ends. Serve coffee, desserts, and plenty of bottled water during this time.
- Make arrangements for employees to get home safely. Offer free cabs and enlist designated drivers. Remember—employers could be on the • hook if employees leave a company-sponsored party drunk.
- Make it a daytime event or family party. Consider serving non-alcoholic beverages only and make it a family-oriented party instead. **(HR360blog)**

I personally recommend against having company parties that serve alcohol, unless its an overnight party and people who drink stay over, ex: in hotels, resorts, etc. In my opinion it is best to provide alternative celebration perks in place of serving alcohol, such as gift cards.

Mistake

NOT PROVIDING HARASSMENT AND
DISCRIMINATION PREVENTION TRAINING
FOR THE ENTIRE STAFF

About 3 years ago, I provided an extensive training session on Anti-Harassment and Discrimination Prevention Training. Two months later, a manager, who had attended the training, pointed out that there was an issue with an employee who, the manager suspected, was harassing another employee. I asked the manager multiple questions, including, "When do you think it started?" The manager answered, "Oh, it started way before you did the training. I know you said to address harassment issues but I didn't want to hurt anybody's feelings and I really thought the problem would go away."

Really???

The Mistake: The mistake is, oftentimes, employers believe employees should have common sense and many times employers expect employees to know how to act properly; especially if the person has extensive education and/or holds a management position. However, this is not always the case. People come from different backgrounds where different behaviors may have been accepted; therefore, we have to make sure employees understand the rules and the consequences. If we do not communicate harassment policies and practices to the entire staff; someone may violate the law and the person being violated may sue the employer.

How to Fix the Mistake: Employee Training is critical in preventing harassment and discrimination; also for appropriately responding to issues when they arise. Employers should periodically train all employees about the harassment policy. Attendance should be mandatory. Training should stress that anyone who believes they or someone else is the victim of harassment should communicate to the alleged harasser that the conduct is unwelcome, if possible, and appropriate. If that does not work, or if the victim is uneasy about approaching the alleged harasser, employees should be given direction of who to report the harassment to and how to proceed.

Does training prevent harassment and discrimination? It may not, however, it will give the employer the ability to discipline properly for harassment violations. Harassment training also provides evidence, when faced with litigation, exhibiting that the employer took action to prevent harassment.

Mistake

072 | MAINTAINING POLICIES **THAT ARE NOT CLEARLY DEFINED**

I've worked with clients who had policies that read a little like the following:

Cell Phones
Employees are expected to use common sense when using his or her cell phone while in company vehicles.

Tuition Reimbursement
ABC Company may provide tuition reimbursement to employees as requested.

Attendance Policy
Employees must be in their work area, ready to work, on time, or they will be written up.

The Mistake: When workplace policies are not clear, employees tend to interpret them in their favor. For instance, in the example above regarding cell phones, employees may think its okay to make calls and accept calls while driving company vehicles. If the employee has an accident, the policy will probably not help, if faced with litigation or vehicle insurance denials.

How to Fix the Mistake: Policies and procedures govern behavior and performance in the workplace. Company and legislative changes make updating policies and procedures essential. Additionally, updated polices may be necessary to address Internet usage, social media, and modified work issues.

Taking the time to write easy-to-understand detailed policies can be the difference in winning or losing at litigation. For example, lets revisit the cell phone policy above. Below is another way to write that section.

Employees who use company vehicles are prohibited from using a cell phone, hands on or hands off, or similar device while driving, whether the business conducted is personal or company-related. This prohibition includes receiving or placing calls, text messaging, surfing the Internet, receiving or responding to email, checking for phone messages, or any other purpose related to your employment, the business, our customers, our vendors, volunteer activities, meetings, or civic responsibilities performed for or attended in the name of the company; or any other company or personally related activities not named here while driving.

Can you tell the difference?

Mistake

073 | NOT POSSESSING AN EMERGENCY CLOSING POLICY AND EMERGENCY EXIT PLAN

I was having coffee with Sydney; we were discussing ways to improve employee attendance at her company. During our conversation, Sydney happened to mention that three months before, all of the employees had to quickly evacuate the premises, due to a large fire in one of the offices. She and the staff were outside for about 2 hours, waiting for the firefighters to clear the building. Sydney further indicated that, while they were outside, she had no way of accounting for the employees. She did not even know which employees were absent or at work that day. "Someone could have been stuck in the building and I would not have known. It was very scary." She said. "It just so happened everyone was okay."

This is not good.

The Mistake: Thinking that there will never be an emergency is a mistake. Things happen. The day could be going great and all of a sudden, boom; a flood, snowstorm, fire, bomb threat, violence, active shooter, etc. Failure to maintain an emergency exit plan can cause a multitude of issues, including unnecessary fatalities.

How to Fix the Mistake: Employers should take the time to think about their workplace and how to deal with emergency closings and emergency exits plans. The Occupational Safety and Health Administration (OSHA) provides an excellent website and booklet full of direction regarding preparing emergency plans and policies. The website is: **https://www.osha.gov/Publications/osha3088.html.** It is a good idea to review the entire website and prepare accordingly.

The OSHA website covers multiple topics, including:

- What is a workplace emergency?
- How do you protect yourself, your employees, and your business?
- What is an emergency action plan?
- What should your emergency action plan include?
- How do you alert employees to an emergency?
- How do you develop an evacuation policy and procedures?
- How do you account for employees after an evacuation?
- What type of training do your employees need?
- How often do you need to train your employees?
- What free onsite consultation does OSHA provide?

I highly recommend perusing this website, or delegating the duty to a responsible employee or manager. The life you save may be your own.

Mistake

NOT TAKING ACTION AFTER
INVESTIGATING
A WORKPLACE ISSUE

Veronica filed a complaint of harassment and age discrimination. She stated in her complaint that Paul, her supervisor constantly referred to her as "old girl." She stated it had been ongoing for approximately 3 years. Veronica stated that she had complained about the problem about one year ago, yet it continued to happen. She indicated that Paul would make nasty comments, such as "Getty up and lets move it old girl."

Veronica shared that she requested a meeting with Paul, one-on-one. During the meeting, Veronica tried to explain that his comments made her feel bad; but Paul's only response was, "Oh suck it up. It's not a big deal. Don't you get paid on time every 2 weeks? Be thankful for that and stop complaining." Veronica said she left the meeting almost in tears. She then filed another complaint with Human Resources the next day.

This time Human Resources investigated the incident and Veronica was told the problem was handled. Well, she filed another complaint about 1 year later citing the same issue. That's when I received a call to investigate Veronica's complaint. While reviewing the background information regarding Veronica's complaints; I was disheartened to learn that, although the issues were investigated, the company failed to follow the recommendations or to take action on Veronica's behalf.

What would have happened if Veronica had decided to seek outside assistance with her issues instead of continuing to file complaints within the company?

The Mistake : Substantiating a workplace allegation after an investigation and not taking action is actually worse than not investigating at all. Not taking action can cause the accused to retaliate and even double up on the harassment, discrimination, etc. against the accuser. Also, the complainant could seek an attorney or file an EEOC complaint citing failure of the organization to appropriately take action. The company could face litigation as well as hefty fines and penalties.

How to Fix the Mistake: It is critical to take action after substantiating a complaint. Employers may be apprehensive about taking action because usually it takes time and resources. Actions typically include: some type of training, Employee Assistance Program (EAP) referrals, updating policies and procedures, corrective actions, etc.

Not taking action can also lead to low employee morale. Employees may feel that the company does not care and that they don't have a valid path to receive assistance with workplace issues. This can cost the employer in decreased production. Therefore, employers should act on validated allegations immediately. If appropriate, remove bad apples, conduct training, etc. Ensure you are providing the actions needed, based on the investigation results, to maintain a high-performing work force.

075 | NOT ADDRESSING FAVORITISM AND
NEPOTISM
IN THE WORKPLACE

A few years ago, while working with a large automotive company, I met and had a conversation with Larry, the Assistant General Manager. I said, "So Larry, what keeps you up at night?' I can still clearly remember what Larry said, "I have problems managing the cleaning crew." He said. We have a team of 20 employees and it's very hard to keep the crew motivated because 2 of them are my Bosses' sons. The Boss will just come down and get them whenever he wants. Sometimes he will come down in the middle of the day and take them golfing, fishing, or to a game. The rest of the crew has to stay the entire shift and oftentimes, have to double up to get the work done. The crew get really, really angry about it; and they get mad at me for not doing anything. But what can I do, he is my boss."

That was a tough one.

The Mistake: Favoritism and nepotism can be bad for business as they cause low morale; which typically leads to a decrease in productivity, which can reduce employers' profits. Favoritism and nepotism can breed discrimination, which is illegal. Title VII of the Civil Rights Act of 1964 protects individuals against employment discrimination on the bases of race and color, as well as national origin, sex, and religion. A claim for employment discrimination must be able to show that an employer's practices disadvantaged employees based on one of those prohibited categories. (Mathis)

In the above scenario, lets assume that the sons are Caucasian. Would there be a case for litigation if the other 18 employees on the cleaning crew were women, or minorities, or disabled? Also, what if the Bosses' intention was to punish the other 18 crew members because they complained about him, and he was angry about it.

Would that be retaliation?

How to Fix the Mistake: Employers should maintain clearly defined nepotism policies. It is also a good idea to avoid having family members supervise each other. Employers that currently have that situation may need to have the employee report to someone else at the company, or if that is not possible, the situation should be closely monitored.

NEGLECTING TO
076 MAINTAIN
DIVERSE WORKPLACE

Yvette, the Director of Employee Relations, explained that she had a few employees who constantly complained about unfair treatment and discrimination. She indicated that the 3 "complainers" were Black men. She further stated that no matter what she and senior leadership tried to do to fix the issues, the men still complained. She was concerned that if this continued, there may be litigation in the future.

Because there was no open complaint at the time, I recommended an HR Audit, which involved reviewing the information and speaking with the three (3) individuals personally. After reviewing the information and speaking with about 12 people, I quickly discovered the problems. All of the management staff and about 90% of the employees were about the same age, race (White), and they pretty much thought about workplace issues in the same manner. When one member of management would leave, they would recruit their friends and associates, which kept resulting in like minds.

Don't understand the problem? Let me give you an example of one of the problems:

A manager at the company asked his subordinate, Joe (one of the "complainers"), where he had been for the last half hour. Joe replied, "I was downstairs helping my sister." Well, the manager was shocked that Joe was working with his sister and did not even know his sister worked at the company. The manager went to his boss and said, "I don't think it's a good idea to have brothers and sisters working so close together." The manager and his boss decided to move the sister to another area.

What's wrong with that, you may ask. Well, it was not really his sister. In Joe's culture, it was common for people to refer to each other as brother and sister, even if they were not blood related. If the company had diversity in management, the reference of "sister and brother" might have been easily explained.

The Mistake: Effective communication is critical to a successful business. Diversity is essential to effective communication. Having a diverse staff, which includes different genders, races, personalities, ethnicities, cognitive styles, tenure, age, education, background, and others such as Lesbian, Gay, Bisexual, and Transgender (LGBT); can set the organization apart through its diverse workforce.

McKinsey & Company and Social Talent provide the following statistics:

- For every 1% increase in gender diversity, company revenue increases by 3%.
- Gender-diverse companies are more likely to outperform others by 15%
- Ethnically-diverse companies are more likely to outperform others by 35%
- Additionally, according to Glassdoor, 67% of active and passive job seekers say that when evaluating companies and job offers, it is important to them that companies have a diverse workforce. Job seekers are drawn to companies with diverse workforces because it is evident that the companies do not practice employment discrimination. (www.mckinsey.com, www.socialtalent.co/blog)

Lastly, diversity in leadership allows managers to bring in new skills and methods for achieving unity within their teams. This can include employing workers with diverse cultural and language skills that can lead to a broader scope and greater reach for business.

How to Fix the Mistake: Let me give you six (6) well-intentioned tips to becoming a more diverse workforce:

- Promote diversity in your mission and communications.
- Create a recruitment strategy with your diversity goals in mind.
- Place job advertisements on diversity-focused publications,

websites, etc.
- Hire an outside HR Consultant or Recruitment Firm to assist with diversity initiatives.
- Partner with diversity-focused groups, the community, colleges, chambers, etc.
- Provide mandatory diversity training, as appropriate.

Also, ensure that staff is engaged in the diversity goals from the top down to ensure everyone feels accepted and welcome.

Mistake

077 | NOT DETERMINING SPECIFIC
TRAINING AND DEVELOPMENT
NEEDS THAT ALIGN TO
ORGANIZATIONAL GOALS

While meeting with a client, he began citing a long list of training and development tools and courses that his company had used to train their employees. After the long discussion, he ended by saying, "but its not working."

The Mistake: When identifying training and development needs, employers often copy other organizations, i.e. provide the same type of training as their competitors, or follow the current training trends. Oftentimes, this practice is a mistake because it does not align with the company's mission and goals. Unfortunately, the company typically spends an excessive amount of resources to train the employees; yet the results are nil.

How to Fix the Mistake: Employees must assess their company needs and goals. Training and development programs should add value, in order to help employees achieve necessary goals. The training should also be aligned to employee performance.

In some instances, management may feel they are too busy to attend training, however, it is crucial to demonstrate the need for training through participation, as well as demonstrate how the training will help the organization. Additionally, everyone at the organization should be on board to support the training and development endeavors.

078

ALLOWING
SR. MANAGEMENT
TO "RUN DOWN THE CLOCK"
TO RETIREMENT

It is surprising to me the number of senior management employees who don't want to make any changes or improvements, because they want to simply complete their last 2 or 3 years of service, prior to retirement, without added projects or changes. Basically, they just want to let everything be until they depart. In their words, "If its not broken, don't fix it" type of attitude. It's unbelievable, however it happens every day.

The Mistake: Allowing a senior leader to "run out the clock" can be extremely costly and a huge drain on the organization. Processes need to be changed, systems need to be replaced, policies must be reviewed, and where necessary updated, etc. In our competitive environment, companies must enlist everyone's cooperation, working to capacity, to ensure maximum efficiency; or suffer draining profits and revenue.

How to Fix the Mistake: HR should monitor workflow and establish succession plans. If the employer discovers a senior leader who is in retirement mode, maybe the senior leader can be moved to a position where he or she can be flexible; i.e., maybe work from home and provide decision-making assistance or historical information, away from the company, until his or her retirement date.

Another alternative is to have someone to work along-side the "soon to retire" employee in preparation to move into the impending vacant position. The main goal is to always keep the organization moving forward.

079 | IGNORING UNEMPLOYMENT CLAIMS

Denise, the Director of Operations of a healthcare organization, was in charge of answering unemployment claims. The organization employed about 4,000 employees; therefore she received quite a few claims. One day, she casually commented to her boss that she hated processing unemployment claims, "But," she said, "I take care of them very well." Denise eventually left the company.

About 2 months after Denise left, someone else was assigned to go through the file cabinets in Denise's old office to scan the files. The assigned employee opened a file drawer and was shocked at what she found. It was filled with unopened letters from the unemployment office, i.e. unemployment claims! The claims dated back over a year.

When I think about this story, I still feel so bad for that employer.

The Mistake: The mistake happens when employers take the position of, "Why bother, the employee is going to get the money anyway. That's just how it is with unemployment." It does not cost employees anything to file a claim; therefore most departing workers will automatically file for unemployment compensation.

Employers have a lot of control over whether a worker receives unemployment compensation. Just because a former employee files an unemployment claim does not mean he or she is entitled to receive unemployment benefits. Once a worker files an unemployment claim, it is up to the employer to timely contest the claim, or, if not, the former employee will likely be grated unemployment compensation.

163

How to Fix the Mistake: There are two (2) factors that dictate whether a former employee will receive unemployment compensation, which are:

1. The circumstances of the employee's departure, and;
2. Whether the employer contests the worker's unemployment claim.

Keep in mind, the higher the number of former employees who collect unemployment benefits, the higher your company costs will be. Therefore, employers should contest unemployment claims appropriately and consistently, in order to save the organization money, by avoiding expensive high tax rates and unnecessary unemployment payments.

Mistake

080

TERMINATING EMPLOYEES
WITHOUT
DUE DILIGENCE

David, the Executive Director, was livid after Casey, a star employee, told him that her co-worker, LaTonya, had been stealing money from petty cash. Casey also said the co-worker was stealing supplies from the backroom. Casey informed David that she and several of her colleagues observed LaTonya stealing the money as well as the items. "As a matter of fact," Casey said, "We believe LaTonya has been stealing items for a few months."

David was furious. He began thinking about LaTonya's past infractions; her being late twice the week before and how she was a no call no show approximately 2 months ago. "She just keeps breaking the rules," he thought. "Well, this is the last straw; she is done!" He then began preparing paperwork to terminate LaTonya. Later that day, David called LaTonya into his office and fired her.

Too bad David wasn't privy to the fact that Casey was upset at LaTonya because she felt that "LaTonya is the reason behind the breakup with my boyfriend." However, David had taken Casey's word because she was a star employee.

What could David have done better?

The Mistake: The mistake is rushing to judgment. Sometimes employers grow tired of chronic rule violators and then they act too quickly by firing them without dotting their I's and crossing their T's. In the scenario above, David could have conducted a quick investigation and interviewed the workers. Firing someone too quickly, without the care that a reasonable person would exercise to avoid harm to other persons, i.e., due diligence, can lead to costly litigation.

How to Fix the Mistake: Unfortunately, there will be times when termination of employment occurs; it is a part of company operations. However, when terminations are handled inefficiently, it can lead to wrongful discharge issues.

Employers should take the time to prepare for a termination; making every effort to avoid any type of litigation. The employee should be treated professionally, with dignity, during the termination process and meeting. It is helpful to follow the steps below:

- Review company polices with the human resources department
- Review the employee's file
- Investigate the issue, as appropriate
- Ensure that the employee was properly counseled and/or disciplined prior to termination for minor violations and performance issues
- Follow discipline process and policies. Be aware of precedent-setting decisions
- Prepare documentation to employee; keep a copy of documentation in the employee file

Remember to do your due diligence before terminating employees.

Mistake

081 | NOT PROVIDING A SAFE **WORKPLACE FOR EMPLOYEES**

In a prior chapter, I discussed, that an employer refused to take action regarding a substantiated harassment investigation. Unfortunately, the validated harassment issue involved several victims/employees. Because the employer did not take action, the harassment grew significantly worse. The employees complained repeatedly via the Complaint Hotline; to no avail.

The Mistake: One mistake is that oftentimes employers believe that a safe workplace refers to injuries, falls, hazards, etc. A safe workplace also pertains to a workplace free of harassment and retaliation. Another mistake happens when employers refuse to take action and assume that problems will go away; or when the employer, or accused, retaliates against the complainants/victims. Retaliation can cause a hostile work environment. In the case above, sadly the victims of the harassment were slowly let go, terminated, one-by-one, by the employer.

Retaliation and hostile work environments can cause the employer to suffer expensive litigation. For example: In 2015, a Federal Judge ordered the US Postal Service to pay an employee $229,228 in damages for whistleblower retaliation; the employee had been subjected to a hostile work environment.

How to Fix the Mistake: Employers are required to provide a safe work place for employees. In 1970, Congress created the Occupational Safety and Health Administration (OSHA) to assure safe and healthful working conditions for working men and women by setting and enforcing standards and by providing training, outreach, education, and assistance. Section 11(c) of the OSH Act prohibits employers from discriminating against their employees for exercising their rights under the OSH Act. (https://www.whistleblowers.gov)

It is best that employers take appropriate action after verifying complaints to avoid harassment and retaliation. Also, Senior Leadership could assign a responsible management committee to monitor complaints and hotlines to ensure complaints are handled properly; and employees are treated fairly. It is also a good idea for employers to monitor the movements of the accused, to ensure subsequent retaliation and/or hostility does not occur.

Additionally, employers should have a well-defined safety plan, which includes harassment and hostile work environment; and the plan should be regularly communicated to employees.

082 | NOT BEING AWARE OF **PRECEDENT** SETTING DECISIONS

In *2014, Peacock Stores -v- Peregrine & Ors*; the employer had, over the years, consistently paid redundancy payments based on statutory terms but without applying the statutory cap on either years of service or the amount of a weekly wage. When the employer wanted to go back and start paying the statutory payment using the statutory calculations, 3 employees complained and brought a claim for contractual enhanced redundancy payments; even though there was no express written policy or procedure setting out how the redundancy payments would be made. The employees relied solely on past custom and practice.

The outcome of the claim was that the employees were entitled to the enhanced terms. The Employment Appeal Tribunal upheld the decision. The employees were able to keep receiving the higher payments due to the employer setting a precedent in which the employees relied upon. **(Reference: Peacock Stores -v- Peregrine & Ors UKEAT 0315/13/SM** - See more at: **http://www. thomasmansfield.com/blog/posts/creating-a-precedent#sthash. oREl5E2S.dpuf)**

The Mistake: The decision to enhance or change a policy, process, procedure, etc., in order to benefit certain employees or to make agreements with employees, could set a precedent for future incidents with employees in similar situations. The change to the policy, procedure, etc. may be a small cost for one employee, but when 100 employees request the same enhancement; it could prove to be costly to the employer.

How to Fix the Mistake: Employers should be cautious when pivoting away from company policies, procedures, processes, etc. If the employer must provide an enhanced benefit to an employee, in order to not set a precedent, the employer should well document the reason why the change was necessary as well as insert a disclaimer that the decision was not precedent setting.

However, if employers are concerned that their previous practices may cause issues for them in the future, a new written policy and procedure, which is properly implemented, can help to make future intentions clear.

Mistake

083 | NOT ALIGNING EMPLOYEE **HEALTH CARE BENEFITS** TO EMPLOYEE NEEDS

"We only offer one medical insurance plan and I can't understand why our costs are so high," said the CEO of an aeronautics company. After reviewing his employee statistics, it was evident why the cost was excessive. 26% of the employees were under 23 years old, 40% were over 55 years old and the rest were in between. Yet, the medical insurance plan was the same for all employees.

The Mistake: In this scenario, although the 23 and under group may not need as much coverage as the 55 and over group, the medical insurance company has to accommodate the older employees and charge the same rate across the board. For example, the insurance may include coverage for colonoscopies, mammograms, etc. Most employees 23 years old and younger will not use those benefits; therefore the organization could be losing money, paying for the same benefits for all employees, which are only utilized by a portion of the staff.

How to Fix the Mistake: It is a good idea for employers to evaluate their employees' health care needs, as appropriate. Employers may be able to retrieve and review a copy of the benefits used the prior year. Employers could also employ the assistance of a Benefits Broker to walk them through the benefits packages as well as the options for alternative plans. In many cases, the Benefits Broker can help the organization save hundreds or even thousands of dollars per month.

084 | NOT PAYING **OVERTIME** APPROPRIATELY

In 2014, Shell Oil Co. and Motiva Enterprises had to distribute massive checks, to more than 2,600 current and former employees, for unpaid overtime; after a federal investigation found that they hadn't been paid to attend mandatory pre-shift meetings. Workers were required to attend meetings before the start of their 12-hour shift. The companies failed to consider the time spent at mandatory pre-shift meetings as compensable; therefore, employees were not paid for all hours worked and did not receive all of the overtime pay for hours worked over 40 in a workweek.

Shell and Motiva agreed to pay $4,470,764 in overtime-back wages to settle Department of Labor (DOL) charges that they violated the Fair Labor Standards Act (FLSA). Additionally, the refineries did not keep accurate time records. The settlement reminds businesses of the importance of properly tracking and paying workers for all compensable hours in accordance with the FLSA and other laws. **(www.Houstonchronicle.com)**

The Mistake: Typically the mistake is not following overtime laws or having a lack of understanding of the laws. Non-exempt employees must be compensated for any time worked during which they performed activities that benefited the employer.

How to Fix the Mistake: The Fair Labor Standards Act (FLSA) requires covered employers to pay non-exempt employees at least the federal minimum wage for all hours worked and overtime pay for hours worked over 40 in a workweek. Some employers believed they didn't have to pay for insignificant or non-regular work, such as meetings or training sessions.

However, 29 CFR 785.27 under the law states:

Attendance at lectures, meetings, training programs and similar activities need not be counted as working time if the following four criteria are met:

1. Attendance is outside of the employee's regular working hours;
2. Attendance is in fact voluntary;
3. The course, lecture, or meeting is not directly related to the employee's job; and
4. The employee does not perform any productive work during such attendance.

Please keep in mind, that wage and hour employment laws make clear that all of the above four (4) criteria must be met. Violations of this law can be very expensive; as shown in the scenario above regarding Shell and Motiva.

Mistake

085 | LACK OF EMPLOYEE **REWARDS**
AND RECOGNITION PROGRAM

A few years ago, I provided HR services for a growing manufacturing company with about 150 employees. The CEO described his company as "highly unorganized with out of control employees." After assessing his organization, I realized that the CEO was not exaggerating.

We had a lot of work to do to get the company on the right track. I personally worked with the company to update policies, streamline processes, implement systems, conduct trainings, etc. We also reviewed company expectations with the employees.

After making the changes, the company began running like a "well-oiled machine." I then said to the CEO, "Now that operations have improved and you have a good team in place; we need to discuss establishing an Employee Rewards and Recognition Program." I was excited about the prospect. The CEO looked at me and said, "No! They should be glad they even have a job!"

The Mistake: Most people like to be appreciated for the work they do, as well as feel that the company celebrates their work. Organizations who adequately maintain an Employee Rewards and Recognition Program typically operate up to 30% better than those who don't have a program.

There are multiple benefits of an Employee Rewards and Recognition Program, which could include:

• Better customer service (employees will feel appreciated and will pass this feeling on to customers)
• Employee competition to do a great job for the company
• Enhanced teamwork
• Increased productivity
• Employees have a sense of pride in their work
• Improved morale and less stress
• Retention of key employees
• Employee satisfaction
• Raised revenue

It is a mistake to not take advantage of the many benefits delivered by having an Employee Rewards and Recognition Program.

How to Fix the Mistake: Some employers may feel they cannot afford the cost of an Employee Rewards and Recognition Program or they don't want to allocate resources to this type of program. However, there are several affordable options to choose from to appreciate employees, such as:

• $5 gift certificate for coffee or specialty drinks
• Certificate of Appreciation in a frame (from dollar store) placed in a

prominent place for all to see
- 2 hours, ½ day, or full day off work with pay
- Postcard from the CEO of the organization sent to employee's home
- Employee acknowledged in the company newsletter
- Gift certificate for dinner and a movie for 2
- Pizza party for the team

With a little creativity, employers can provide a stellar program to appreciate employees.

Mistake

086 | MICROMANAGING STAFF

About 7 years ago, I received a call from the CEO of a telecommunications company. Rodger, stated the company was having issues with employee absenteeism and Family and Medical Leave Act (FMLA) abuse. Rodger indicated that the call-offs were negatively affecting his business. He said he had tried everything to improve the issue by changing the policies and implementing a perfect attendance incentive; yet it continued to happen. I told him that it would be my pleasure to assess his organization.

After observing and speaking with several managers and employees, the problem became very apparent; the Operations Manager, George, was a micromanager. George was all over his employees. He moved from workstation to workstation all day, monitoring everything his employee did on the job. George was watching and monitoring employees so much that they could barely go relieve themselves without permission. Hence, the cause of the excessive employee absenteeism problem was discovered. Found it!

The Mistake: Merriam-Webster Dictionary Online defines the term "micromanage" as: "to try to control or manage all the small parts of (something, such as an activity) in a way that is usually not wanted or that causes problems". It seems as if Merriam-Webster knew George. **(https://www.merriam-webster.com/dictionary/micromanaging)**

In most cases, micromanaging staff can cause multiple problems in the workplace and can negatively affect operations and revenue. It can cause employee stress, which can lead to illness and/or lack of confidence. It can also produce:

- Low morale
- Feelings of resentment
- Lack of trust
- Employee Turnover
- Lack of creative and free thinking
- No self-motivation and independence
- Low productivity, i.e., working slower to not make a mistakes

As you can see, micromanaging can prove very costly to the organization; and can get even worse if not addressed.

How to Fix the Mistake: There are a few ways to address the issue of micromanaging. First, it may be a good idea to evaluate the manager to ensure he or she is a good fit for a manager position. Not all employees make good bosses. Other solutions could include:

- Assertiveness training for the manager
- Delegate more responsibility to the manager
- Conduct teambuilding exercises based on trust
- Train the manager on delegation techniques
- Because micromanaging can be extremely costly to the organization, it is probably crucial to address the issue as quick as possible. It may take a little time to change the behavior, however, it will be well worth the effort in the long run.

087 | NOT KEEPING TRACK OF AND **FINDING SOLUTIONS TO** **WORKERS COMPENSATION** CLAIMS AND ISSUES

Colleen was the Housekeeper at a nursing facility. She made a habit of telling her coworkers, and almost anyone else who would listen, that she despised her job; and she was only working there because her husband was out of work. One day, Colleen approached her manager and indicated that she slipped while mopping and hurt her arm. There were no witnesses, however, due to the alleged injury, Colleen stated she had to have surgery. She was placed on workers compensation.

Every summer, like clockwork, Colleen would tell her boss that she had to rest her arm and it could take 2 – 3 months for her to be ready to work again. The facility would approve her for workers compensation payments to cover her time off work. This went on repeatedly for several years.

Is there anything the employer could have done to not incur that cost? Maybe.

The Mistake: It is a good idea for employers to work closely with their legal counsel to determine their options when it comes to workers compensation claims. In the above scenario, the employer did nothing to alleviate the situation; therefore it probably won't take long before other employees want to jump on the bandwagon, i.e., "me too". Thereby, it could get extremely costly for the employer.

How to Fix the Mistake: Along with working with legal counsel and/or workers compensation specialist, insurance company, and human resources; the employer should make sure the employee's physician has a copy of the employee's job description to determine if the employee could work with or without restrictions; if possible. The employer could also have a pre-arranged work situation for employees who need accommodations.

However, to avoid litigation, it is best to work with a workers compensation specialist, the employer's workers compensation insurance company, human resources, and/or legal.

088 | NOT POSSESSING A
SOCIAL
MEDIA POLICY

According to the New York Times, when 2 employees of a famous restaurant filmed a prank in the restaurant's kitchen, they decided to post it online. In a few days, thanks to the power of social media, the employees ended up with felony charges, more than a million disgusted viewers, and a major company facing a public relations crisis.

In videos posted on YouTube and elsewhere an employee prepared sandwiches for delivery while putting cheese up his nose, putting body fluids on the sandwiches, as well as violating other health-code standards while a fellow employee provided narration. The two were charged with delivering prohibited foods.

As the restaurant realized, social media had the reach and speed to turn tiny incidents into a marketing crisis. **(https://www.nytimes.com/2009/04/16/business/media)**

The Mistake: Not educating employees regarding social media online posts, videos, etc. can be a costly mistake. The restaurant in the above scenario had to spend an excessive amount of money in marketing to save their reputation and also had to close down the store for a cleaning overhaul.

How to Fix the Mistake: Employers should create and maintain a social media policy. The policy should educate employees and clarify the values and culture of the organization. A well-written social media policy can:

- Protect the organization's reputation
- Guard confidential information
- Provide a contact person to assist employees with social media by answering questions about what is appropriate
- Explain to employees how to engage with others online
- Communicate what is legal and not legal
- Discuss social media usage that violates organizational rules

All of the above can save employers considerable time and money. Equally important, such policies will create a better work environment for both the employer and the employees.

It is also important, however, to have assistance when drafting a social media policy and when disciplining an employee for posting comments on a social media site. Otherwise, an employer could violate Section 7 of the National Labor Relations Act (the "NLRA"), which applies to both union and non-unionized work forces. It states: *"Employees shall have the right to...... and to engage in other concerted activities for the purpose of collective bargaining or other mutual aid or protection."* An employer that disciplines an employee who engages in "concerted activity," or an employer that posts a broad social media policy prohibiting such protected activity, violates the NLRA and may also violate 29 USC §158(a)1.

For example, it may be illegal for an employee to post online that the employer's product or service is bad, but it might not be legal for the employee to post that his or her hours are bad.

089 NEGLECTING HIGH- PERFORMERS

"We've lost 4 high-performing employees in the last year. It's really hurting us." said Arthur, COO of a transportation organization. "What have you done to try to keep them?" I asked. "We treat everyone the same. Don't want to be sued for discrimination or favoritism." Arthur said.

He may have missed the point...

The Mistake: Not listening to the needs of high-performers may be a huge mistake. High-performing employees are key to organizational success. They are also oftentimes hard to find, as they are few and far between. Employers miss valuable opportunities when they ignore high-performer's needs and treat them the same as a low-performers. If the high performers leave, the employer may have to replace them, which is costly as well as the possibility of suffering an unfortunate drop in productivity and/or efficiency.

How to Fix the Mistake: It is important to ensure high-performing employees have varying and interesting work responsibilities. Employers can also consider incentive programs, such as productivity goals, to reward the employee for their work. If there is room for growth, employers can promote those directives throughout the organization. Employers can also work to help develop high-performers.

Employers can create policies to provide flexibility incentives to award for high-performers. Employee surveys can also be used to assist in determining and developing programs and motivations. If a high-performer decides to leave, it is a good idea to meet with him or her to find out why he or she is leaving and, if possible, make an offer to try to keep him or her.

You can avoid discrimination and favoritism allegations by ensuring all employees have the opportunity to achieve the same incentives as well as the ability to climb the corporation/organizational ladder, by providing the same opportunities as the high-performer.

090 | PLACING WORKERS IN **MANAGEMENT POSITIONS** FOR THE WRONG REASONS

About 2 years ago, while presenting my findings from an HR Audit to the CEO of a transportation company, I recommended that the company hire a Director of Operations to oversee business activities. The CEO, Helen, agreed with my recommendation and assured me that she would proceed with my recommendation. About 3 weeks later, I stopped by to speak with Helen and she was very excited. "We have a Director of Operations!" "Wow!" I said, "How did you find someone so quickly?" "Oh, I just gave the position to my friend Roland. He was laid off from his factory job," Helen said. "I know he is not really qualified, but he did take 1 or 2 business classes last year and he really needs my help. He should be able to learn the job."

I wish Helen would have consulted with me first. Needless to say, it was a bad decision that turned out to be disastrous.

The Mistake: Recruitment is the process of generating and attracting a pool of **qualified** applicants for organizational open positions. The most important step to recruitment is aligning the employer's business strategy to its recruiting strategy. It can be crucial that employers hire applicants that can "hit the ground running" and who are highly-qualified, in order for the organization to realize their investment right away. In most cases, hiring unqualified individuals can be costly to the organization in loss of productivity, low employee morale, and expensive replacement costs.

Additionally, according to a Gallup study, hiring the right people for management roles represents the single greatest opportunity facing organizations today simply because of the upside it signifies. The study indicated that managers account for 70% of the variance in employee engagement scores. When a company raises employee engagement levels consistently across every business unit, everything that matters to an organization's long-term viability gets better. (Gallup)

How to Fix the Mistake: Hiring great management talent takes time and planning. Employers should take the following steps to facilitate hiring the right management staff for the right reasons:

- Review your mission, strategic plan, goals, and needs
- Create an ADA compliant job description
- Make sure the recruiter or human resources representative understands the job needs
- Find out where the best managers for the job can be found (i.e. what publications do they read, which websites do they peruse). Post your jobs in these areas.
- Spread the word to your associates that you are looking for great manager, director, etc.
- Write interview questions based on the job description
- After the interview, try to only consider candidates who are qualified and who will be the best fit for the organization.

Also, according to Monster.com, 92% of the best people don't find their jobs via job posts online; they find them through some type of referral or they've been recruited. Therefore, it is a good idea to promote the management position using various methods, such as hiring an HR Consultant or search firm.

ASKING EMPLOYEES FOR TOO MUCH
091 | MEDICAL
INFORMATION

The Assistant General Manager, Harold, requested my assistance with his Family and Medical Leave Act (FMLA) issues. When I met with him, I asked Harold to explain the issues and to describe what he had done thus far regarding the problems. He told me that one of his employees went on FMLA leave, and he was very upset. He indicated that it seemed that the employee would be off 2 weeks and then come back and be off 2 days. Harold felt that the time off was not warranted. So he said he met with the employee.

"I tried to be calm." He said. "But I was tired of her nonsense. I told her I wanted to know specifically why she was off work and how long she had the condition. I required that she bring in a doctor's note for every absence. I also called her doctor. Well, she finally exhausted her FMLA." And it went on from there.

Not only was Harold probably subjecting the company to FMLA interference, he was most likely asking for too much medical information.

The Mistake: The mistake is requiring employee to provide too much medical information. For example, according to the **EEOC website**, in 2015, PAM Transport, Inc. was ordered to pay $477,399 to 12 of its former truck drivers in a lawsuit brought by the EEOC. In the lawsuit, the EEOC alleged that PAM violated the Americans with Disabilities Act (ADA) by subjecting its entire workforce of truck drivers to overly broad medical inquiries.

The lawsuit arose from PAM's medical clearance policy, which required all drivers to notify the company whenever the driver had any contact with a medical professional, including a routine physical. Such alleged conduct violates the ADA, which prohibits employers from making medical inquiries of employees unless the inquiries are job-related and consistent with business necessity. **(https://www.eeoc.gov/eeoc/newsroom/release/3-4-15b.cfm)**

How to Fix the Mistake: Employers must ensure that their medical inquiry policies and practices are job-related and consistent with business necessity, as required by federal law. For FMLA, employers can request medical certification, but must tread lightly when asking for other medical information to ensure to not ask for too much information. The safest course of action, to verify the existence of a serious health condition, is through the Department of Labor's FMLA forms for that purpose. Employers typically can ask the employee to have his or her own doctor complete the certification.

Regarding the American's with Disabilities Act (ADA), employers can request medical certification of disabilities covered by the ADA; however should restrict requests to the situation at hand, namely, the nature, severity and duration of the impairment, the activities it limits, and the extent to which the employee's activities are limited, and why the requested accommodation is needed. Employers should not ask for other health information and should not ask at all to certify conditions that are obvious. For example, an employee in a wheelchair should not be asked to provide medical certification of the need for a wheelchair ramp.

IGNORING
092 | MORALE
ISSUES

I clearly remember, several years ago, when I worked with a company that had the lowest employee morale that I had ever witnessed. I probably observed 50 or 60 of the employees and I don't remember any of them smiling, or appearing happy. Fortunately, I had the opportunity to speak with several of the employees and it became very evident that there was a problem; on a fairly large scale.

One of the employees, Jaylen, told me, "Sometimes I am ordered to go to the bosses houses and do work. I don't think that's right. I signed up to work here. If I do it, I get treated well, but if I don't do it, I have to walk on eggshells at work, so I don't get written up. Also, if the boss is in a bad mood, which is most of the time, he sets the stage for the rest of us." I heard stories like this from employees over and over again.

Thankfully, I was able to work with management, and we were able to dramatically improve the morale at the organization.

The Mistake: Merriam-Webster Online Dictionary defines morale as: *the feelings of enthusiasm and loyalty that a person or group has about a task or job*. Morale is the employee's attitude and perception about his or her job, the work environment, the co-workers, management, and the organization overall. Signs of low morale include:

• Turnover,
• Increase in employee and customer complaints,
• Rise in absenteeism,
• Escalation of employee conflicts and disagreements,

- Decreased productivity; etc.

Low morale is costly to the organization and can keeps organizations from operating optimally.

How to Fix the Mistake: High Morale is crucial to organizational success. If low morale is witnessed, it should be addressed immediately. In most cases, happy employees mean happy customers, which can mean increased revenue.

The following strategies can be used to improve low morale:

- Allow employees flexibility, if possible
- Encourage independence, innovation, and creative thinking
- Communicate well with employees
- Get rid of bullies and bad apples
- Eliminate micromanagers
- Conduct teambuilding exercises
- Address complaints timely and take action if needed
- Conduct employee surveys
- Make employee jobs as interesting as possible

In most cases, employees want to enjoy their jobs and have a comfortable place to work. Low morale should be addressed. It also helps improve morale when management listens to employees and works diligently to resolve issues as quickly as possible; to show the employees that they matter.

Mistake

093 | LAYING OFF OLDER EMPLOYEES TO
H I R E
YOUNGER EMPLOYEES

According to the **New Jersey Law Journal**, in January 2017, a federal jury in Camden issued a verdict that would require Lockheed Martin Corporation to pay $51.5 million, including $50 million in punitive damages, in an age discrimination suit by an engineer, according to court records. The suit claimed Lockheed Martin had a practice of laying off older employees while hiring younger workers for the same position. The Plaintiff, who held the title of Project Specialist, senior staff at Lockheed Martin's facility in Moorestown, filed suit after he was included in a reduction in force at the facility in July 2012, when he was 66. Out of 110 employees at the Moorestown plant with that title, five were laid off, including Braden. All five were over the age of 50.

Additionally, according to **Los Angeles Daily News**, in 2014, a Los Angeles Superior Court awarded a 66-year old man, $26 million in an age discrimination lawsuit against Staples Inc. In what an attorney called the largest award of its kind in Los Angeles legal history, the jury found that he was discriminated against and harassed based upon his age by his supervising managers at Staples. Nickel's claim cited instances of harassment, derogatory name-calling and wrongful suspension from managers who tried to intimidate him into resigning.

Currently, at the time of this writing, General Mills and HP Inc. are facing claims of age discrimination by multiple employees.

The Mistake: The Age Discrimination in Employment Act (ADEA) prohibits discrimination against people with disabilities in employment. Per the **Equal Employment Opportunity Commission,**

age discrimination involves treating someone (an applicant or employee) less favorably because of his or her age. The ADEA only forbids age discrimination against people who are age 40 or older. It does not protect workers under the age of 40, although some states do have laws that protect younger workers from age discrimination.

Violating the ADEA (without a job-related or other reasonable exception allowed by law) can be extremely costly to the organization, as shown in the cases above.

How to Fix the Mistake: Employers should take precautions when laying-off or retiring older workers. Per the **EEOC: ADEA Fact Sheet,** an employer may ask an employee to waive his/her rights or claims under the ADEA either in the settlement of an ADEA administrative or court claim or in connection with an exit incentive program or other employment termination program. However, the ADEA, as amended by the Older Workers Benefits Protection Act (OWBPA), sets out specific minimum standards that must be met in order for a waiver to be considered knowing and voluntary and, therefore, valid.

In order to protect the organization, retaining legal counsel to assist with lay-offs of older workers may be a good way to proceed, before implementing the lay-off.

189

Mistake

094 | NOT ISSUING TIMELY
COBRA
L E T T E R S
TO SEPARATED EMPLOYEES

While working with an organization, I asked the Office Manager, "May I review a few of your COBRA letters for the HR Audit?" She replied, "I try to get them done, but most times I'm just too busy to keep up with the COBRA letters."

Immediately I say to myself, "This is not good…"

The Mistake: Keeping up with COBRA (Consolidated Omnibus Budget Reconciliation Act) notices and correspondence can be a daunting task for many employers. However, unfortunately, it's not uncommon to find this duty neglected. Even if the employer uses a third party administrator (TPA), the employer should ensure the notices are administered appropriately.

For example, in the case Pierce v. Visteon Corp., Visteon, a large global automotive supplier, outsourced its payroll, benefits and COBRA administration processes to a number of different TPAs. Over the course of several years, many separated employees failed to receive their COBRA notices. A class-action complaint against Visteon was initiated and, when all was said and done, the court awarded statutory penalties of $2,500 per affected participant, 741 former workers, which added up to $1.8 million in total penalties. And that didn't include attorney's fees. (https://ecf.insd.uscourts.gov/cgi-bin/show_public_doc?12005cv1325-300)

How to Fix the Mistake: COBRA requires covered plans to provide employees and dependents with notification of their rights to COBRA coverage on the occurrence of certain events. Employers should be aware of the Notice and Election Requirements, which include:

- Employers must notify plan administrators of a qualifying event within 30 days after an employee's death, termination, reduced hours of employment or entitlement to Medicare.
- A qualified beneficiary must notify the plan administrator of a qualifying event within 60 days following the event.
- Plan participants and beneficiaries generally must be sent an election notice not later than 14 days after the plan administrator receives notice that a qualifying event has occurred.
- The beneficiary then has 60 days to decide whether to elect COBRA continuation coverage.
- The beneficiary has 45 days after electing coverage to pay the initial premium.

For more information, to ensure compliance with COBRA requirements, employers may review the COBRA Fact Sheet at: **https://www.dol.gov/sites/default/files/ebsa/about-ebsa/our-activities/resource-center/fact-sheets/fsCOBRA.pdf.**

095 | LACK OF HAVING AN
EMPLOYEE
ASSISTANCE PROGRAM

While working onsite at an automotive company, Kaleb, the IT Specialist, asked if he could speak with me. I told him I was on my way to meet with the CEO and asked if we could talk later in the afternoon. As I was talking with him, I noticed a strange look in Kaleb's eyes. So, I called to reschedule the meeting with the CEO and I then met with Kaleb.

Kaleb said, "Vanessa, my wife left me 2 days ago. I am so hurt and depressed. I am a recovering alcoholic and a month ago I started drinking again. I have not had a drink today, but I am felling really bad. I don't know what to do? I am having a hard time coping."

Employee Assistance Programs can be beneficial with these types of situations. Thankfully, the company was able to assist Kaleb in getting the help he needed.

The Mistake: Partnering with or maintaining and Employee Assistant Program (EAP) can be invaluable to the organization's employees. The EAP can actually help protect the organization by intervening and assisting employees who are experiencing emotional distress, mental issues, substance abuse, etc. and attempt to find a solution before the problem becomes unmanageable. Clearly, it's easier to treat an emotional issue early on then it is when it is out-of-control.

How to Fix the Issue: An Employee Assistance Program (EAP) is a voluntary, work-based program that offers free and confidential assessments, short-term counseling, referrals, and follow-up services to employees who have personal and/or work-related problems.

It is recommended to consider maintaining or contracting with an EAP program. It is estimated that troubled workers make up between 10 – 15% of the workforce, and they tend to have higher rates of absenteeism and on-the-job-injuries. These workers are often less productive than other employees, and are heavier users of costly health benefits. Therefore, a well-designed EAP program can assist companies with solving employee problems, reduce health care costs, and as an alternative to psychiatric care; which is good for the employees and for the bottom line.

096 | FAILURE TO PROVIDE MEANINGFUL
WORK WITH
A CLEAR PURPOSE
IN MEETING
ORGANIZATIONAL OBJECTIVES

Natalie, the Intake Manager of a non-profit organization, was complaining about two of her employees. "Corrine and Janay are always arguing about their work. They race each other to try and get the easier projects and fight (not literally) over the simpler accounts. I am tired of intervening and having to solve their conflicts. Their work is always behind and yet they complain about the workload." I listened carefully, and then asked, "What are their job titles?" Natalie replied, "They are both Intake Clerks." I then asked, "How long has the job existed?" Natalie answered, "Those jobs have been around forever, at least 10 years."

I asked Natalie to describe the job duties. While she was discussing what the job entailed, I almost fell asleep from boredom. The jobs were unexciting and some of the duties were obsolete. I remember thinking, no wonder they argue. They are trying to make their jobs more exciting. I suggested that I work with Natalie to restructure the jobs and make the jobs more motivating with attainable goals. It took us a couple months, but we were able to create new, more interesting jobs for both employees.

We then met with the employees and explained the new jobs as well as the positive impact of their new jobs on the organization. Immediately I could see the employees' expressions change to one of excitement.

So far, it has turned out well...no more conflicts!

The Mistake: Failure to provide meaningful work with a clear purpose is a missed opportunity for employers to excite and motivate employees about their work and the organization. Most employees want to feel like their job matters. In most cases employees who feel their job is valued and they are needed, achieve better productivity results; which can help the organization's bottom line.

How to Fix the Mistake: Employees want to see how their work contributes to larger corporate objectives, and setting the right targets makes this connection obvious for them, and for the employer. Employers can review the jobs and evaluate the meaning and purpose of the job. It is ideal to communicate the purpose of the job as well as its positive impact on the organization. Just think about it, most employees want to feel valued and they typically get motivated when they have a purpose and are making a difference to the organization.

097 | LACK OF HAVING A **SUCCESSION P L A N**

"Many of our employees in key positions have been here for more than 20 years. It's going to be tough when some of them retire." stated by the HR Manager of a health care organization.

The Mistake: Succession planning is the ongoing process of systematically identifying, assessing, and developing organizational leadership to enhance performance. Succession plans are designed to identify and prepare candidates for high-level management positions that become vacant due to retirement, resignation, death, or new business opportunities. Recognizing that changes in management are inevitable, employers should establish a succession plan to provide continuity in leadership and avoid extended and costly vacancies in key positions. (Mathis)

How to Fix the Mistake: It is in the best interest of employers to assess leadership needs of the organization to ensure the selection of qualified leaders are diverse and a good fit for the organization's mission and goals and have the necessary skills required. Employers can establish a Succession Plan Committee to facilitate succession planning.

Typically, the succession plan can be established via the 7-steps below:

1. Identify critical positions
Critical positions are the focus of succession planning efforts.

Without these roles, the organization could be unable to effectively meet business goals and objectives.

2. Keep an open Mind
Although some successors may seem obvious, it is crucial to not disregard any promising employees. Identify employees who best display the knowledge, skills, and abilities necessary to perform, and thrive, in the position, regardless of his or her title.

3. Identify competencies
A clear understanding of capabilities needed for successful performance in key areas and critical positions is vital for guiding learning and development plans, setting clear performance expectations, and for assessing performance.

4. Identify succession management strategies
The next step is to choose from a list of options of several human resource strategies, including developing internal talent pools, onboarding and recruitment to address succession planning.

5. Provide training to peak performers
Conduct and provide training and mentoring to facilitate development of new skills and refine existing skills.

6. Document and implement succession plans
A documented succession action plan provides a tool for clearly defining timelines, roles and responsibilities.

7. Evaluate Effectiveness
To ensure that the department or agency's succession planning efforts are successful, it is important to systematically monitor workforce data, evaluate activities and make necessary adjustments.

Succession planning can really be a good thing for the organization, however, it is important to ensure there are no violations of the law, such as discrimination, retaliation, etc.

098 | SENDING IMPROPER **E-MAILS** TO EMPLOYEES

Below is an excerpt from an actual email sent from a Director to an employee (the employee was not his direct report):

Do you know what your role and responsibilities are as the Marketing Specialist? I don't think you have a clue. You continue to drop the ball. As the Director of Housekeeping, I will contact you directly concerning anything I want. If you have a problem with this file a complaint. You cannot determine who can and cannot contact you. If you do not want me to contact you, you should look for another job!

Here's another one from an employee to her manager...

...and you constantly pick on me. I know that you don't like me and I don't know why. Is it possible you don't like me because I have a different skin pigmentation than you?

What problem do you see with the above emails?

The Mistake: E-mail communications can be considered "evidence," and can be used against employers in a lawsuit, in the same manner as any other written letter, document, or memorandum. Employee email messages can be submitted to courts as evidence in claims of discrimination, sexual harassment and other illegal activities. Also, remember, deleted emails may be able to be recalled, and an improper message can come back to haunt an employer, months or years after the message was initiated. Needless to say, inappropriate email transmissions can be extremely costly to the employer.

How to Fix the Mistake: It is highly recommended that employers establish an effective email policy. The email policy should establish expectations for the entire staff, and should include:

- Reminder that emails are to be used for company business only
- How to handle confidential information
- To not send emails that may contain text that is considered discriminatory, offensive, insulting, condescending, abusive, personal attacks, sexist, racist, or considered harassment
- To refrain from sending political views, unless it's a business necessity
- To not forward inappropriate emails
- The consequences/penalties for sending and/or forwarding inappropriate emails

The email policy should include other expectations as aligned to the organizational requirements. Employers should then monitor emails and take disciplinary action against abusers, as appropriate. Lastly, employers should avoid sending emails when angry.

Mistake

099 | FAILING TO ADEQUATELY PROCESS ACCRUED VACATIONS TIME UPON TERMINATION

While meeting with the Director of Human Resources at a financial services company, he indicated that the company rarely paid vacation accrual to employees, and stated in order for employees to receive their accrual, they had to be outstanding and give at least two months or more notice; that way the company could replace the employee before the person leaves." "It saves us money by having the leaving employee train the new employee; and we need at least a month for that. So, the leaving employee gets like a bonus."

Really?

The Mistake: Typically, the mistake happens when employers are not aware of their state law regarding payment of vacation accruals. According to **Workplace Fairness**, 24 states—Alaska, Arizona, California, Colorado, Illinois, Indiana, Kentucky, Louisiana, Maine, Maryland, Massachusetts, Minnesota, Nebraska, New Hampshire, New York, North Carolina, North Dakota, Ohio, Oklahoma, Pennsylvania, Rhode Island (after one year of employment), Tennessee, West Virginia, and Wyoming—and the District of Columbia have laws regarding payment of accrued vacation time.

In the rest of the states, there is no state law that requires employers to pay accrued vacation leave; although employers may do so voluntarily, or may have to do so if required by a policy or contract. **(http://www.workplacefairness.org/final-pay#3)**

How to Fix the Mistake: Employers should be familiar with their state laws regarding vacation time accrual. Also, it is recommended that employers maintain clearly defined policies regarding vacation accrual pay, describing how it will be paid to the leaving employee, upon termination; or how it will not be paid; or other outlined option as chosen by the employer (as long as the option is allowed by law).

100 | IGNORING POLITICAL **CONVERSATIONS IN THE WORKPLACE**

Please note: This mistake does not apply to organizations where political conversations are business-related.

The Mistake: When employees are allowed to discuss politics in the workplace, tempers can flare and productivity can suffer. It takes only one person to have an inflammatory discussion, which can alienate someone or cause a hostile work environment or potential harassment claim. Additionally, the conversations could become aggressive and violence could ensue. Therefore, employers should ensure the organization is protected.

How to Fix the Mistake: It is recommended that employers review the following steps regarding politic discussions in the workplace:

1. Ensure Managers are trained to avoid political conversations/discussions in the workplace and during working hours. Managers set the tone for the workplace and employees typically take their cue of what is acceptable to discuss at the workplace from management.
2. Communicate to employees the detrimental effects of political conversations and advise them to use discretion. Let employees know that people have different views and that political conversation has the potential to create a hostile work environment and/or may offend someone. Let the employees know that the organization supports diversity.
3. Establish and/or review policies. To create a respectful work environment, make sure your Anti-harassment, Discrimination
4. Prevention, Retaliation, Non-solicitation, Political Activity, and

Loitering policies are maintained and up to date. Ensure to communicate those policies to employees.

5. Ban political slogan buttons, T-shirts, etc. as part of your dress code policy, particularly for employees who come into contact with clients or customers. Make sure the ban is company wide, including senior management and owners.

6. Avoid political endorsements and comments, other than offering a statement to employees encouraging them to be socially responsible and vote.

Please note: Regulating political discussion is a tricky balance as discussions of minimum wage, equal pay, paid leave — things that affect working conditions — might be protected by federal labor laws. On the other hand, careless comments about race, gender or religion could also lead to harassment or discrimination claims.

Mistake

101 | FAILURE TO BUY AND R E A D THIS BOOK!

Reading this book could potentially save your organizations thousands, hundreds of thousands, or millions of dollars. Keep your workplace protected!

Sources

Sources for this book included:

- Equal Employment Opportunity Commission
- Code of Federal Regulations (EEOC)
- Mathis, Robert L., Jackson John H. – Human Resources
- Mondy, R Wayne, Martocchio Joseph – Human Resources
- HR360
- Uniform Guidelines for Selection Procedures (UGESP)
- US Department of Labor (DOL), Wage and Hour Division (WHD)
- US Department of Labor Fact Sheet #17A
- IRS.gov
- Workplace Bullying Institute
- Society of Human Resources Management (SHRM)
- US Department of Labor's FMLA Advisor
- Huffington Post
- LA Time Online

About the Author

Vanessa G. Nelson is founder and President of award-winning Expert Human Resources, which she created in 2009 to help companies maintain employment law compliance, avoid workplace litigation, maximize human capital, create great teams, and reduce costs.

Vanessa is a results-oriented HR Professional with a unique background in business management, spanning over 29 years at two major corporations in Michigan. She has successfully helped many organizations save millions of dollars via her consulting and expertise, which includes: HR audits, management training, workplace investigations, executive recruitments, compensation studies, management coaching, labor relations, policies and procedures.

Ms. Nelson conducts seminars and speaks all over the United States, and is known to be relaxed and easy-going, but serious when it comes to improving organizations.

Vanessa's clients include: McDonalds, Henry Ford College, Genesee County 911, Mass Transportation Authority, Bedford Public Schools, Old Newsboys, Genesee District Library, Detroit Wayne Mental Health Authority, Valley Area Agency on Aging, and Saginaw Transit Authority Regional Services.

Vanessa is very involved in the community and is currently the HR Advocacy Captain for Congressman Dan Kildee and the 5th Congressional District. She is also the President of newly formed Elite HR Professionals Association (SHRM affiliate). In the past, Ms. Nelson served as President of the Women's Leadership Committee for the Flint and Genesee Chamber of Commerce (2013 – 2015) and served as President of the Mott Community College Alumni Board (2013). Additionally, Vanessa provides seminars for the community, including *Top 15 Costly Mistakes Made in HR...and How to Fix Them*, at various venues.

Vanessa has also composed multiple E-books and workbooks, including: ***Do-It-Yourself Employee Handbook, How to Write Employee Documentation that Could Stand-Up in Court!, and 7-Simple Steps to Conduct an HR Audit Today!***

Academically, Vanessa achieved her Master's Degree in Human Resources Management from Central Michigan University; the Senior Professional in Human Resources (SPHR) credential from the Human Resources Certification Institute (HRCI), Senior Certified Professional (SHRM-SCP) from Society of Human Resources Management (SHRM), and Certified Labor Relations Leader (CLRL) from Michigan State University (MSU).

55191451R00120

Made in the USA
San Bernardino,
CA